Faith and Perseverance – My Journey

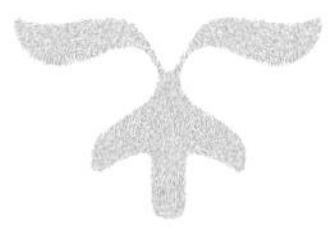

Kiran Joshi, Ph.D.

Faith and Perseverance – My Journey
Kiran Joshi, Ph. D.

© 2023

Cover Art by: Niyati Bedekar
Maps by: Amrin Bhangu

ISBN: 979-8-218-24104-9

FOR INFORMATION, CONTACT:
KJoshiAuthor@gmail.com

: Dr.Kiranjoshi_

www.KiranJoshiAuthor.com

Printed in the USA by:
Morris Publishing
3212 US-30, Kearney, NE 68847

Kiran Joshi, Ph.D.

TO MY LOVING PARENTS

I am who I am because you sacrificed!

TO MY DEAR FAMILY AND FRIENDS

Life is so beautiful because you are in it!

Kiran Joshi, Ph.D.

Table of Contents

Kiran Joshi, Ph.D.

Map of INDIA with Insert of Punjab (Map 1)

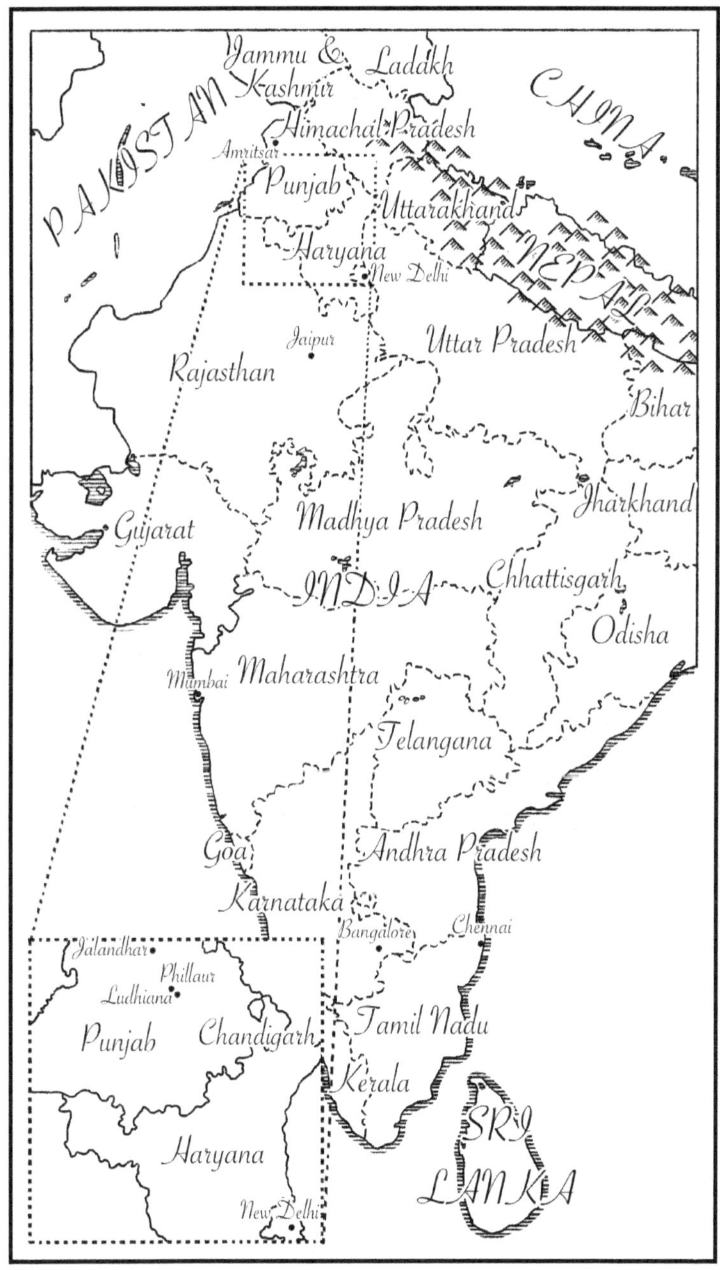

Map of BRITISH COLUMBIA, Canada (Map 2)

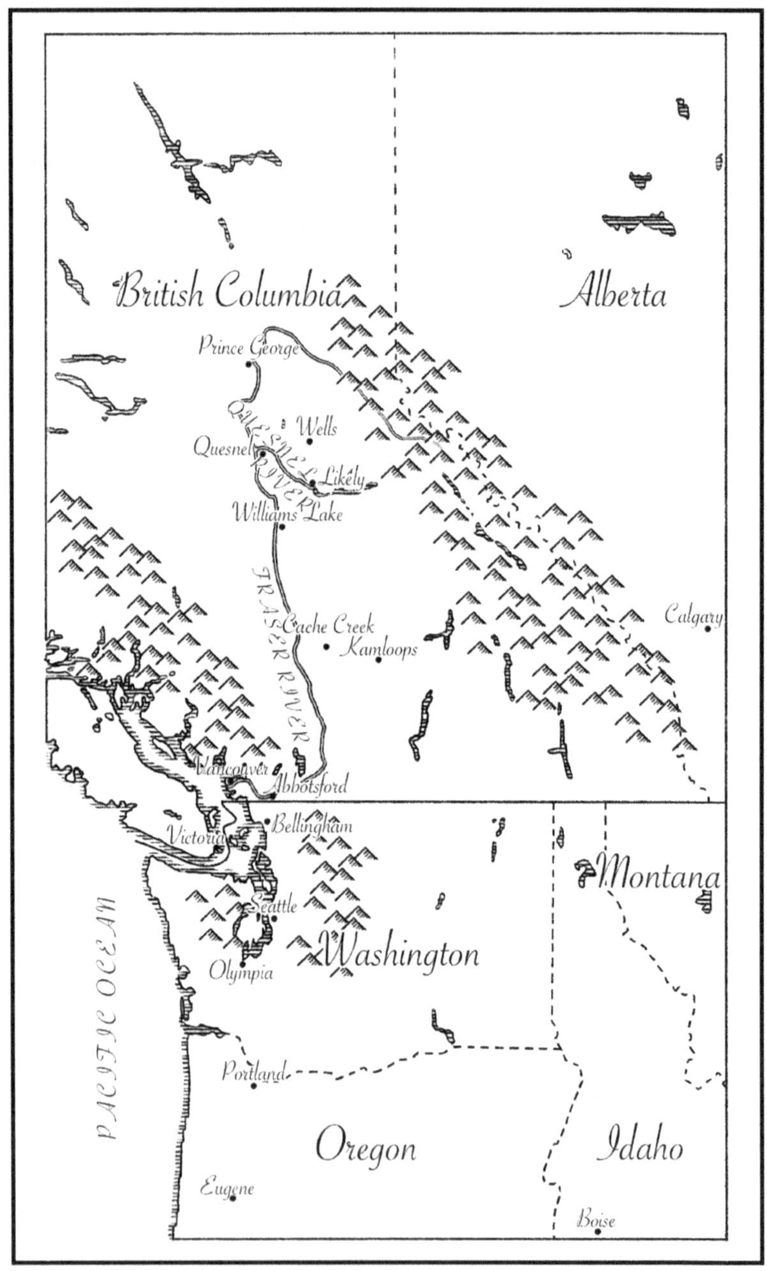

Kiran Joshi, Ph.D.

INTRODUCTION

The cycles of birth, death, and re-birth will keep on going until life has taught us what we need to learn. Although we work hard on controlling outcomes in our lives to ensure that the positive experiences outweigh the negative ones, what if we allowed the life to unfold itself while not clinging to certain outcomes? How do we relate to ourselves and fellow human beings when a life-threatening illness or hard times land at our doorstep? Do we allow these events to define our life, or do we use these as opportunities to grow spiritually?

We face such questions throughout the journey of our lives. If we take the time to reflect on both pleasant and unpleasant circumstances in our life, we might notice that all experiences fit perfectly. We had to go through them to become who we are today. We may also notice that difficult times and experiences help us recognize and develop our inner strength if we slow down enough to reflect on these moments.

The inspiration for this book comes from people who are close to me, and from some that I have been in touch with but never met in person.

Kiran Joshi, Ph.D.

The questions from fellow human beings on my cancer journey are many. The first set of inquiries is from people who saw me going through cancer treatment but tell me that I do not speak about what it was like to go through it. Another set of questions is from people who have been diagnosed with cancer and are trying to figure out the path forward. The caregivers or relatives and friends of people who have been diagnosed with cancer also want to know what lies ahead for them and their loved one. Then, there are some cancer survivors who are interested in knowing how to put this saga behind them mentally and move ahead without this disease controlling them. Finally, I get asked about what gave me strength to get through cancer without complaining. It appears that life was preparing me for many years to deal with cancer gracefully by setting me on a spiritual journey from an early age.

At my workplace, young or prospective moms often ask how I managed motherhood and the career. Some of my colleagues are interested in knowing how I ended up in my current role of Environmental Protection, Worker Health, Occupational Safety, and Sustainability (EHSS) after getting a Ph.D. degree in chemistry. Some people are curious about the path that I took to reach the executive position that I am in now.

Faith and Perseverance - My Journey

All these inquiries are tied to my spiritual path, the story of immigration from India to Canada as a teenager, and the sacrifices that my family made to get me to college. When I give people my responses, I often get asked to write these down.

My journey of life may not be much different or remarkable compared to many. Every up and down in life has taught me gratitude, love, patience, and perseverance. I am immensely grateful for all that life has offered me, and I share some experiences here.

Kiran Joshi, Ph.D.

1. WHEN CANCER KNOCKED AT MY DOOR!

It was early July 2012 when I first felt something hard in my left breast. My loving husband and I were on our way to Mendocino from San Jose, California, for our 24th wedding anniversary. I so vividly remember asking him in the hotel room if he felt something in my breast, and he did not. I too stopped feeling, thinking, or worrying about it. The routine of life took over for six more weeks. Along came mid-August. While showering one Friday evening, the long hard lump in the same breast could simply not be ignored. I asked my husband once again. His words were, "You better call your doctor on Monday." Our niece was with us from Canada that weekend. She and my daughter were so excited about spending time together; being around their liveliness took away the fretting and worries of the lump.

Monday morning rolled along, and I called the doctor. My appointment was late in the evening the same day. After meeting with me, the doctor and the nurse had worrisome looks on their faces. They wanted me to get the mammogram done as

Kiran Joshi, Ph.D.

soon as possible, but it was too late that day. The following day, I was dressed up for work in a dress that I still own, stockings, and brown sandals. I went to the clinic for the mammogram from work. For this scan, I was asked to remove the dress and wrap a paper gown around me. Once the mammogram was done, I was sitting in the waiting room along with few other women feeling almost naked in my gown, stockings, and sandals. It seemed like a long wait, but no one looked at or talked to each other as we all likely had the same feeling of nakedness combined with the dread of the upcoming news. After the mammogram was complete, the technician directed me to get an ultrasound scan done the same evening, which I was not expecting. The clinician conducting the ultrasound scanned over the hard lumpy region of the breast repeatedly. I looked at the screen and I clearly saw a long band which was black while the area around it was not. The dark region appeared dead to me while the lighter areas around it were alive. As I dressed to leave, the nurse handed me pamphlets related to breast cancer.

Every step was taking me closer to the reality that I had breast cancer. There was no sense of panic or anger during this time; in fact, I was in disbelief. How could it be that I had breast cancer? There was no history of this illness of which my family members were aware. The immediate thought arose that it was likely the chemical use during graduate school that messed up my DNA!

What came next pushed me along in time. It was a slew of tests including a biopsy and appointments with various specialists. The biopsy was quite painful as needles were inserted into the breast to extract some tissue samples. I kept mentioning to the physician doing the work that I was in pain. He did not seem to pay a whole lot of attention until I broke down in tears. Only then he stated that one of the needles was likely resting on a nerve ending. He tried to move the needles a bit to provide some relief, but his attitude towards my complaint seemed quite callous. I was wheeled from one room to another by a nurse with tears flowing due to the pain. Although it felt like a long time, the procedure ended after 15 or 20 minutes. I was relieved of the misery.

A few days later, I was in a work meeting when I received a cell phone call from a different physician. I walked out of the meeting to take the call. The female voice said, "Mrs. Joshi, I am sorry to tell you this on the phone that your biopsy revealed that you have breast cancer." I vividly remember that conference room and where I stood outside in the corridor. I thanked her and went back to the meeting. I still felt no fear or anger, just a neutral set of emotions. I continued on with the meeting and the rest of the day at work without saying a word to anyone. I told my husband about the confirmation of cancer after dinner was done.

The next step of notifying family and friends was done that evening and over the next few days. People were shocked that I had cancer despite a healthy lifestyle of a vegetarian diet, minimal alcohol, and little sugar consumption, as well as exercising five days a week. Neither was I showing any physical signs of an illness brewing so silently. Later, I commented to the oncologist during one of my appointments about all the healthy habits I had lived by, and asked why these did not help in preventing cancer. Her comment was that I would have gotten cancer ten years earlier if I had not lived such a healthy lifestyle.

When I first met with the oncologist, I did not panic or have any upsetting feelings. She described to me that, since there was no family history of breast cancer, surgery to remove the tumor and close monitoring afterwards would be sufficient. In addition to the tumor removal surgery, she scheduled me to meet with the geneticist, which I did reluctantly. I sat through that meeting barely even listening. I did not ask any questions of her as my mental state was, "Naha, it is not genetics related; I do not need to listen to this." I kept going to work as there was a month before the tumor removal surgery. Colleagues commented that I looked too calm knowing that I had breast cancer. I don't really know what one is supposed to look or act like after getting such a life-altering diagnosis!

A month later, the tumor was removed, and that's when tough times started. I got a call from the surgeon a few days after the surgery asking me to come in as he found more tumors than expected from the scans. He also wanted to discuss the results of the genetic analysis done on the tumor that was removed. My husband and I met with him. The news was that I had Stage 3 metastatic DCIS (Ductal Carcinoma *in Situ*) breast cancer which was linked to BRCA1 (*Br*east *Ca*ncer Gene *1*) gene mutation. Now that was scary – not as much for me as I was in the thick of it but for my children. Coming to terms with the fact that the cancer was not due to chemical use but due to genetic mutation was difficult. It meant that this cancer would not end with me. BRCA1, in fact, is a gene which produces proteins to help repair damaged DNA. If a harmful variant of this gene is inherited from a parent, the risk of breast and ovarian cancer, along with a few other cancers, goes up considerably compared to the rest of the population, in both men and women.

On our drive back home, we stopped at a coffee shop where we both stayed in a somber mood. That shop is still there, and I remember the two of us just sitting there without having much to say to each other. During the drive home and frequently thereafter I kept thinking, what if the test result was wrong? What if my test sample got switched with someone else's? Then the realization would sweep over me that the result was likely not wrong because the surgeon found several smaller tumors in the breast tissue also which were not expected to be there! I had been doing periodic breast exams, prescribed mammograms, and annual pap smear tests since my mid-twenties. Nothing was ever detected in the mammograms, although my pap smear report was abnormal a couple of times. Upon repeating the pap smear test, it would be normal. How could this be? How could it go from "nothing wrong" to "Stage 3" metastatic breast cancer just like that? I was on this emotional rollercoaster for several days as I digested and accepted this news.

While we made our way home from the coffee shop, my husband still did not say much, but his worried face told the whole story. He did not need to verbalize anything.

I came home from the appointment feeling quite dejected. As I walked into the house, my dear mother, who had joined us to help during this tough time, came to the door to tell me that we had run out of milk. She asked if we could pick some up from a store before removing our shoes to come inside the house. Ooh, that was a moment – I had no desire to hear about what we had run out of at home! My world was falling apart, but how was my mother to know what I had been told? Lack of milk at home felt so insignificant compared to what lay ahead of me, my children, future generations, and other women in the family. My husband told my mom later that day that she could just make a list of what was needed at home for him to get later in the day.

The atmosphere around the house was subdued as the days passed with little sound of laughter. My darling husband's reassurance that we would get through it together was all I needed to hear, though. He stood by me every step of the way without ever sharing his fears or showing his emotions, even when I asked. This trait of equanimity is in his genes as I have never seen him or his parents get overly excited or upset about any situation. They still act from the place of care. If my partner had shown his fears and concerns, it likely would have alarmed me.

One day, with tears flowing, I told him that he did not sign up for this when he married me. He looked at me and took me in his arms; he assured me that he would be by my side no matter what came our way. I fully trusted him. My mother moved in with us from Canada for many months while my father came for a few weeks at a time. My family members started calling

Kiran Joshi, Ph.D.

regularly. Friends started coming more often, sometimes with meals, which lifted our spirits.

Although we had told my parents and close relatives of the diagnosis from the beginning, we did not tell our children of the genetic mutation. We did not want to worry them with more than what they already knew. One day, when my daughter and I were driving home from a doctor's appointment, she asked, "Mom, why do you need all these surgeries?" I explained to her about the BRCA1 gene mutation and the associated risks. She pulled the car off the highway to a side road and parked. She began to cry and told me that she was not upset for herself that she may have this mutation; instead, her tears were for what lay ahead for me. We hugged each other and cried together until we were spent. After half an hour or so, we drove home in silence. She started watching movies with me as we laid together in the bed on certain days while she held my hand. The intensity of our bond was so deep during these moments; we were two bodies yet one soul as my pain was also her burden. She asked what I needed from her during this challenging time – my request to her was to stay focused on school and graduate from the university on time. And she did.

I simply do not think that the severity of the situation fully registered with our son as he was young, but he certainly knew that something was wrong. I wanted him to talk to me and interact with the rest of the family, but he withdrew to his room and spent time with his young yellow Labrador dog. (He had forced us to get this dog for him in 2011. Since we already had a Pomeranian dog, we were not ready for another dog. He was adamant that he needed a dog that he could go out for a run with.) This dog was exactly what got him through those months of my cancer treatments as all the attention at home was on me. Daily dog walks also became the time when my son and husband were able to be open with each other. I do not know what conversations they had, but I was grateful when it was just the three of them together for a few minutes outside the house.

My mother focused on her work around the house and distracted herself with the Indian soap operas on television. She never showed her emotions to me, but deep in my heart I knew that she prayed and cried privately in her room. My husband was the same – he did not show or share his fears with me even when I asked him; he remained cheerful, for my sake and to keep the family going.

Our Pomeranian dog, who previously had not been attached to me at all, started following me around the house. It was peculiar how she trailed me through the house and sat in the bathroom while I took a shower. It was like she knew that something was not right, and she was doing her part by watching over me. She stopped this behavior once all my treatments were finished.

Another visit with the geneticist was added; this time, I was listening! She explained the elevated risks of future cancers related to BRCA1 gene mutation. A hysterectomy had to be done due to high risk of ovarian cancer which she termed a "silent killer." She described the elevated risk of another breast cancer also unless I underwent mastectomy. But first, there was chemotherapy to get through. The oncologist prescribed eight treatments of chemotherapy.

A decision had to be made if I would continue working during chemotherapy or if I would take medical leave. I decided on the latter as it would give me time to focus on the recovery. There was someone else at my work who was undergoing chemotherapy a few weeks ahead of me. She sat across from me at work, and I had seen her crying and looking thinner by the day. Based on what I saw, I wanted to focus only on one thing at a time and decided that it was time to put the professional work on hold for as long as it was needed. I remember thinking, "Let us get through this." The entire regiment of treatment and surgeries ahead became a huge project to get through.

The last day of work was a day before chemotherapy. That evening, my husband picked me up from work and we drove to the hospital to get the infusion port installed. The next day was the first treatment; my husband drove me to the infusion center. Within minutes of the infusion starting, I could feel the coolness of the beet-colored burgundy liquid in my body in addition to the metallic taste on my tongue. Hours passed at the center. Before the first infusion, I was prescribed a litany of pills for controlling nausea, inflammation, anxiety, and for sleeping. I used only antinausea and anti-inflammation pills. Regardless of taking the antinausea pills, the nausea kicked in within 48 hours of the infusion. My joints started aching within a day or two as my whole body got inflamed. A day after the infusion, my dear friend drove me back to the clinic to get a shot to boost my immunity. She took on this responsibility for the next seven sessions. My daughter, when home from college, and other friends stepped in to drive me and stay with me during the next rounds of infusion. What a community of dear ones! All this eased the burden on my husband.

After every infusion, I would have a craving for a Subway vegetable sandwich with whole wheat bread. I was not a Subway frequenter before this time. My companion and I would stop at one location near the infusion center and then head home. My mom would have something cooked to hand to the person who accompanied me. This was a kind gesture that we all appreciated.

After every treatment, my mouth broke out in boils. Constant gargles of salt and baking soda water soothed them. The taste buds died after the first infusion. Food tasted bland and chalky. As the second infusion happened, the oncology nurse recommended that I shave my head as my hair would start falling out soon due to effects of the chemo. My husband and I walked into a hair salon that weekend and requested both of our heads shaved. We had a chuckle out of seeing our bald scalps in the mirror when the hairdresser was done with shearing us. When we returned home, my mother was so sad to see us with shaved heads, since according to Hindu customs, a son shaves his head only at the parent's funeral. The lack of hair did not phase me at all, though. My already balding husband decided to keep his head shaved going forward. Even while growing up, I had short thin hair. Hair was not something that I missed. I, in fact, liked the beauty of my bare skull. I bought some scarves and a wig to wear when I stepped out of the house. I hardly ever used them. The eyebrows, eyelashes and other body hair thinned as the weeks passed.

As I progressed with the infusions, I went for daily walks in the neighborhood even when there was so little energy left in this body. There was one moment I was standing in a window looking at the outside world when the thought came to me that I understood the meaning of "dead man walking!" Although this phrase is used in the American prison system when a condemned prisoner is being taken to his execution, at that moment, I felt like I was almost dead yet still alive. The infusions were every two weeks. The first week of every infusion was rough from nausea, joint aches, boils in the mouth, and the lack of energy. The second week would be better in terms of these symptoms; then I would get ready for the next infusion. This went on for sixteen weeks. The smell of the infusion center became a nausea trigger over the weeks.

One day during the infusion, I overheard a nurse asking a patient in the next compartment if she had someone to drive her home after the infusion. Her response was inspirational as she said, "I am ninety years old; I drove myself here, and I will drive myself home." Wow! Although I admired her, I also felt immense gratitude for my daughter and girlfriends for driving me and sitting with me for the infusions which made many hours go by fast. However, I could not help wondering if cancer were to return, at what age would I decline the treatment?

Kiran Joshi, Ph.D.

Everyone makes their own choices. I am sure that I too will do that if faced again with a cancer diagnosis.

Due to low immunity during chemotherapy I stayed at home, other than going out for walks. My partner did all the outside chores such as grocery shopping. Some days, I would feel such an urge to leave home that my dear husband would take me out for a drive on the scenic Pacific Highway. The sight of the Pacific Ocean would make me feel so heavenly. Although my partner had a full-time job, he did his best both at home and work when I made requests for long drives during weekdays. It must have been hard for him to say "no" to me, but he never let it show. His managers were understanding and allowed him during this time if he needed to be away.

On the doctor's advice, I stopped eating raw food such as vegetables, salads, and fruit without peels. I also stopped going to the gym to keep public exposure limited. Walking and reading were the best activities during this time. Due to low energy, my walks were so slow that elderly people would pass me by. This always made me chuckle. Sometimes, while on a walk, I would see young moms playing with their toddlers which would warm my heart.

There were certainly bad days emotionally during this time when the thoughts that I might die from this would cross my mind. I never felt any fear as it was the only certainty that we were guaranteed in life, but the thought of not seeing my children grow older or not meeting my grandkids used to bother me. Thinking about my children having to evaluate for BRCA1 gene mutation used to suffocate me from time to time. As years have passed, I am not affected as much by the thought of my children testing positive as there will be better detection and treatments if they need to face it.

During one visit, a friend asked if I ever question "Why me?" My response which came from nowhere surprised me – it was, "Why not me; there is nothing special about me." I did not know that I had such strength until I uttered those words. It felt like it was not me talking; there was someone else behind me that was speaking through me! It is hard to explain. Perhaps the Buddhist teachings have clarified for me that the cancer was of the body, not the soul! If the body's nature is to fall ill, it will fall ill. And there is nothing more to it.

My husband and my mother did everything around the house and that was immensely helpful. I just wish that I was kinder to my mother. Years earlier, during happy times, my dad let it slip while praising my achievements that my mom was not ready to have another child when she found out that she was pregnant with me. My brother was only two at that time, and she wanted an abortion, but he would not let her get one. One day during the cancer treatments when I was at my lowest point, I lashed out and told her that it would have been better if she had aborted me! I regretted my words the moment they left my lips, but such harsh speech could not be taken back! These words had the power to hurt and hurt they did! Understandably, she became terribly upset and told me that I could never ever begin to fathom what she was going through watching me suffer! She left for her room and cried for a long time. Many years later, I apologized to her for my comments and some of my behavior during that time, and her response was that she did not remember any of it. Only a mother could be so loving and forgiving!

Although many of my girlfriends became even closer to me during this time as they stepped into the role of drivers, sitters, listeners, entertainers, and meal providers, there were some who totally disappeared. Let alone the visit, not even a phone call or a note! It certainly bothered me during that time. Once, out for a walk during the chemo treatments, I ran into one of them. She did not know what to say to me even then. She departed quickly after saying that she would call. Of course, she did not. These missing friends and I became close again when I re-entered their world after several months. Just like with death, people simply may not know what to say to a cancer patient. Perhaps, a simple note that I am thinking of you or get well soon might do! Deep in my heart, I never held a grudge against them as I cherish them deeply.

Once when my dad was visiting during this time, I offered to take him to the Gurudwara (Sikh Temple) near our house. He refused. This left me perplexed as he read the Sikh holy book called "The Guru Granth Sahib" routinely, along with listening to Gurbani (teachings from the Sikh holy book) and meditating. I asked my brothers why he would not want to visit the Sikh Temple. Their response was that he was upset with his "Gods" for causing his daughter so much misery! I did not know what to think of this comment. These were his feelings, and we honored them. He did not show his emotions to me as he was always jovial in my presence. I suspected, though, that my illness was the topic of discussion when my parents were alone.

My dear relatives called, visited, and kept me going. Although it was a tough time, I do not remember being angry, feeling sorry for myself, or being bedridden. Instead, the whole experience felt like a huge project that I had to get through one step at a time. I dealt with the task at hand. This was certainly my defense mechanism that got me through without falling apart. In front of me, my husband was stoic and even keeled during this time. A friend recounted afterwards, however, that he was misty-eyed when she inquired about my health.

There were some funny times too during these months. An incident that stands out in my mind is one day of pooja (prayers) when I was wearing a wig on my shaved head. As a ritual in the pooja, rice was thrown on the attendees. Some grains landed on my wigged head. Instead of struggling with removing the rice from the hair one grain at a time, I removed the wig, shook it out, and put it back on my head again. This led to some laughter from me and others for sure.

Although chemotherapy was the hardest treatment I went through in my life, I still maintained a healthy diet. Being vegetarian, most of my diet was around beans, lentils, whole grains, and vegetables which was not much different than before except that it did not include raw vegetables, salads, and fruits without peels. My dear father used to make me pomegranate juice while my mother focused on cooking Bengal Gram and spinach which were high in protein, iron, and other nutrients. On the doctor's advice, I had stopped taking multivitamins and other supplements such as calcium during chemotherapy since she did not want any interference. So, a healthy diet was much needed.

As life would have it, I had bought Jack Kornfield's book called "The Wise Heart" from the East West Bookstore in Mountain View just before this all started. I read it from cover to cover during these months. Although the book is filled with wisdom, what stayed with me was Jack's own recovery from the trauma of living in a house filled with violence. His teaching of freedom of heart under any circumstance was powerful for me. It made me realize that the cancer was the illness of my body, not my soul, which was freeing. This book led me to read "The Tibetan Book of Living and Dying" by Sogyal Rinpoche, along with others on similar topics. The Tibetan Book of Living and Dying was difficult to comprehend during the first read. Repeated study of it, however, has opened me to the nature of mind, being present in this life, the role of karma, taking care of the dying, my own death and rebirth. Now, I look forward enthusiastically to re-reading this book and learning something new every time. These books opened the entire world of Buddhism and loving heart for me.

The completion of chemotherapy treatments took sixteen weeks. Despite low immunity, with the precaution of staying isolated, I did not catch any infections. Although chemo was behind me, the surgeries were next. Due to the elevated risk of ovarian cancer, a hysterectomy was to be done. It was scheduled a month after the last chemotherapy treatment, allowing me to gather strength. I was also able to bring my vitamin D levels up which had been depleted during the chemotherapy. Since the organs scheduled for removal were not visible, the trauma of getting the hysterectomy was not there. I already had two wonderful children who were heading towards adulthood, and I viewed this surgery as another major milestone in the project that I was handed by life. It was a laparoscopic procedure, and the surgeon felt that I did not need to stay overnight in the hospital. The nurse wanted me to start walking slowly a few hours after the surgery. When I took my first step, I doubled over with pain. The pain was so excruciating right above the navel that I was kept in the hospital overnight anyway. The surgeon suspected that tissues above the navel were likely torn during the insertion of the laparoscopic probe. I lay in the hospital bed that night with a kind nurse holding my hand. She told me that she was Jewish and had certain gene mutations due to her heritage. She said that she would also be going through all these surgeries after having her baby. I still remember her utmost kindness as she sat with me the entire night just talking. I was released the next day.

Full recovery took four weeks. During the first week of the recovery, I used to wake up with hot flashes which lasted a few days but were manageable. My body had been placed in sudden menopause from the hysterectomy.

One surprise from this surgery was a $50,000 bill from the El Camino Hospital since the surgery room or the overnight stay had not been booked. If my memory serves correctly, it was the former. This was my first glimpse of the American medical insurance system. I called the health insurance company along with the surgeon's office questioning this charge. Apparently, the insurance company had approved the hysterectomy procedure but not the location of the procedure. This makes one wonder what the thought process was behind this! Where would the surgeon conduct the surgery? When people are going through difficult health issues, having to deal with insurance problems is the last thing they should have to encounter! Eventually, the bill was cleared without me having to pay anything.

During this time, I was receiving long-term disability payments from the State of California fund that I had contributed to while I was healthy and working. At one time, these payments stopped. When I realized that a few weeks later, I called the disability office. The person on the other end asked if I received a letter asking me to recertify if I was still disabled. I told him that I did not remember getting that letter. His comment was that if I could not keep track of my mail, it was not his problem, and he hung up. It felt like such a betrayal that made me angry since, during my healthy years, I had contributed to this fund and his paycheck. I was turned off and did not care for any further benefits from this office. This was a system that was not working for people when they needed it. I fully understood that such systems do get taken advantage of by some, but I was not doing that, and this person on the other side of the phone line had no compassion. This upset me. I was so devoid of energy already; I had nothing left in me to call this office again.

A month after the hysterectomy came the double mastectomy. The geneticist had described the chances of getting another breast cancer in the same breast and/or in the other breast. She was not adamant about mastectomy compared to hysterectomy; monitoring was an option that was given to me. I did not want to have to deal with another cancer if I could avoid it, though. I decided on a double mastectomy so I could wrap up the project. Some friends thought that I was going to the other extreme with this decision. Why not just monitor? I was in no mood to live with the fear of another cancer event and chemotherapy along with mastectomy down the road. Although I made the decision, it was painful to come to terms with it as the surgery day got closer. After all, breasts define a woman's femininity. By this time, I was also quite exhausted from chemo and other surgeries. When meeting with the mastectomy surgeon, I was firm that I was not interested in the breast reconstruction surgery two months after the mastectomy. The surgeon was a kind woman who explained to me that she understood but most women eventually did want the reconstruction done as our breasts defined us as women. Unless she inserted the breast implants during the mastectomy, I would need an additional surgery to get the implants placed below the skin at a later point. I reluctantly gave in at that time.

The mastectomy was early in the morning. The night before, I gave my breasts a long look in the mirror and shed some tears. In hindsight, I wish I had taken their photos! The surgeon arrived. After the pleasantries were over, she started to draw contours with a sharpie where she would remove the breast tissues. Tears started to flow again. This was the only surgery during which I cried. I was released within a couple of days. I went home with these squeeze bulbs hanging out on each side of my chest to remove the fluid buildup throughout the day. Upon the doctor's advice, I had rented a reclining chair from a medical supply shop, which was a life saver. I rested and slept in it for a month as it allowed me to get in and out easily without having to put weight on my chest. My chest wall was so mutilated after the mastectomy that it was difficult to look at. The pictures of mastectomy that I saw on the internet did not do justice until it was staring me in the face.

After a few weeks, the surgeon slowly started filling the inserts with fluid to expand the chest wall. It was a weekly visit for the fills; the first couple of days after every fill, it felt uncomfortable as the skin was stretching. Once I reached the fills which would have given me size thirty-two chest, I stopped. The surgeon tried to convince me to go a couple of sizes higher; she commented with a bit of naughtiness on her face and in her voice, "Do you not want to show a little cleavage?" It made me laugh, as I was not a chesty person to begin with. And after all this suffering, being able to show cleavage was far from my mind.

Now, eight months had gone by in order to get through lumpectomy, chemotherapy, hysterectomy, and double mastectomy. Breast reconstruction and the infusion port removal were next; these were two months away.

Before I leave the treatment and surgeries, I must acknowledge that the surgeons, specialists, physicians, nurses, and clinicians who took care of me during this ordeal at Palo Alto Medical Foundation and the El Camino Hospital were top notch and empathetic. Nothing was missed, and the whole treatment and surgeries were done as clockwork. I ended up with no infections or reactions to any procedure due to their diligence. We tend to forget the operations staff behind the scenes that makes it all happen. I have a deep gratitude for them as well. It was also abundantly clear how hard the nursing staff worked to take care of me and other patients under their care. The surgeons and doctors came and went, but the nursing staff was the engine that kept the patients taken care of. What a noble profession health care is! I also felt deep gratitude about being in a Western country like the United States where I could get this treatment. Advances in medicine have come so far; how can one forget the scientists and engineers who have made these discoveries in drugs, and technology possible, and will continue to do so in the future!

Such illnesses are hard on the caregivers as all they can do is be there wholeheartedly and lovingly. My family fortunately stood steadfast by me as they suffered silently watching me suffer. Such hardships can test the strength of relationships where not all marriages survive. I feel very fortunate to have a supportive partner and family. At times, I cannot help but wonder what I would do if I were placed in the role of a caregiver! I am hopeful that I will not have to find that out with my children! If I were to provide care for a family member dealing with cancer, I would not want to recount my experiences with them. Instead, I would want to be fully present to listen to what they were going through. I would not show my fears, and I would encourage them that they had a lot to live for. I would bargain my life with the "Heavenly Gods" for their protection.

While working on this book, I asked some of my loved ones what they were thinking during my cancer treatment. (I did not ask my parents as they are in their 90s, and it did not make sense to take them back to the painful time.) The common answer was that they were scared that I might not survive this. Some also described how helpless they felt about the pain I was in. My son shared these comments which touched me deeply: "Witnessing my mom undergo breast cancer treatment was a profound and indelible experience that fundamentally altered my perspective on life. Being young, I was unable to fully grasp the gravity of the situation unfolding. My mom never showed nervousness or fear for the situation due to the calm strength she exuded. I was also never scared or nervous. I recall the household being steeped in an atmosphere of restrained tension, the kind that felt like a held breath. I remember feeling a disconcerting blend of helplessness and determination as the situation was beyond my control and I wanted to support her in every way I could. Amidst all this, there was a maturity that bloomed, a sense of resilience and empathy that was born out of hardship. I learned to cherish every shared moment and to find joy in the simplest of things fueled by the hope and courage my mom displayed every day." I was in tears after reading this paragraph from my son.

My daughter told me that she tried several times to write something down, but she could not take herself back to that time. Some other family members also chose not to share their feelings because it was painful for them. As my family supported me unconditionally and lovingly through this time, I feel a deep sense of gratitude for them. I wish the same support from family, friends, and communities for those who fall on hard times. I also want to make myself fully available when someone needs me. A friend advised me before chemotherapy started that I should just sign up one friend for each infusion to drive me and sit with me. For many of us, asking for help is difficult and seen as a sign of weakness. I had to make myself vulnerable during this time by allowing others to take care of me and embracing it. Every time I visited the oncologist, she asked about the support at home. In hindsight, if someone did not have

Kiran Joshi, Ph.D.

the support, did the clinic offer some resources? I wonder! Is that why she was constantly inquiring? I truly hope so.

I cannot help but wonder if the cancer showing up in me has something to do with the move to the western world. I do not know which side of the parents this gene mutation came from, but no women from either side who live in India or in the western countries have been diagnosed with breast cancer. Is it the western diet, stress, and other environmental factors such as chemical exposure in the research labs during graduate school and the postdoctoral fellowship which triggered the BRCA1 gene to initiate cancer in me? The geneticist did encourage my parents to test for BRCA1 gene mutation so that the women on that side of the family could be notified, but their physician in Canada discouraged them from this test due to their age. He did not want them to take on any unnecessary burden. I see both sides of the advice. It is quite possible that the women in the family chose not to disclose it even if they did get cancer due to the stigma attached to this illness in the Indian culture! I have notified the female relatives on both sides of the family. As far as I know, none of them have been tested for the gene mutation. It saddens me. Although breast cancer is survivable if caught early, ovarian cancer may not be as merciful.

I am aware that what I described above may affect someone's decision on cancer treatment, but I have learnt that the human body has an innate ability to heal and to keep us alive. I have also learnt how precarious yet wonderful this life is. It is worth living no matter how hard cancer treatment is to get through. After sending cancer off in remission with determination and perseverance, I refuse to let it control me. It is not easy, but reminding myself that I have beaten it once, and I will do it again if needed gives me strength. Why worry about something that is not here? The mantra that anything can happen to anyone at any time gives me the ammunition to appreciate what is here now. Every day when I am with my loved ones in good health is a blessed day. I do not take life for granted anymore.

Now that the chemotherapy and majority of the surgeries were behind me, stepping back into the world was ahead. Just the eight-month gap seemed like ages when I went back to work.

Kiran Joshi, Ph.D.

43

2. KAL KHEL MEIN, HUM HOAN NAA HOAN...

"Kal Khel Mein, Hum Hoan Naa Hoan.
Gardish Mein Taare Rahenge Sadaa..."

The title line of this chapter is from an old Bollywood Movie called "Mera Naam Joker (My Name is Joker)!" by R.K. Films, 1970. It translates as follows: It does not matter if we are in the game of life tomorrow or not, the stars will still be orbiting. When I returned to work, I expected the workplace and people to be exactly where I left them eight months ago. But I had a rude yet powerful awakening!

The first day back was interesting. What hit me the hardest was that people and the workplace moved on simply fine without me. It was also a lesson that we tended to think how important we were at work, but the workplace survived. I certainly realized that people died all the time; the world did not stop moving forward due to their absence.

Kiran Joshi, Ph.D.

Within a few hours of being back at work, an executive officer of the company approached me to tell me that one employee who used to report to me would no longer be doing so because of the downsizing of the company. My first thought was that could it not wait until tomorrow after I had some time to catch up! I was focused on myself only. Others who had gotten more visible to the management because I was not there at all commented, "We didn't expect you to come back in full capacity." And, "We were hoping that you would find a job elsewhere since there was a good opening down the street from the current business." It all made me feel sad. Although it took a bit of getting used to the fact that some might be equally fine if I did not return, colleagues and employees were supportive and happy to see me.

As I reflect on my feelings in a larger context, what would I say if I were in these employees' shoes, as my emotions above were based only on my thoughts of self-importance? These individuals had their own priorities. These were good people who were not trying to hurt me by any means. What I might say to someone who has returned to work after a serious illness might be quite different though! Regardless, I did not hold on to any hard feelings towards these individuals as time passed since we were all reacting from the place of what mattered to us. As I became more grounded over the next few months, it was clear that holding on to these hard feelings was the poison that was only hurting me! I did not want to carry it with me as I lived on. Over time, I also learned that my response to any situation was under my control. I did not have to catch whatever ball was thrown at me. It was ok to let it drop.

In hindsight about the overall ordeal, I would not change a whole lot about how I handled the cancer saga. Keeping the emotions out and dealing with it as a challenging project worked for me. Although we do not get to redo our lives, if I could change anything, there are two things – First is that I may not opt for double mastectomy and take my chances with another bout of breast cancer. Losing the breasts affected me badly both mentally and emotionally and continue to do so to some extent even now. During the most intimate moments with my husband, I often feel the lack of these body parts although he has never treated me any less than a complete woman. Secondly, I would take more time off from work instead of just one month after the double mastectomy. I used to be very tired at work for many weeks after I returned. There was a bench under a weeping willow tree next to a lake nearby which became a resting spot in the sun while I gathered my strength. I remember even dozing off on this bench from time to time while the Canadian geese and the ducks hobbled around me. A few times, mama ducks would pass by with the line of their ducklings behind them which was always a pleasant sight to watch. Life was renewing itself as spring arrived, and so was my body.

The best part after the surgeries was being able to eat raw vegetables and fruits again. A salad never tasted so delicious as it did the first time after eight months of not having it! Why do we not eat or drink so mindfully that it is the first time of tasting that food or drink every time we consume it? Why do we forget so easily once the difficulty has passed? My taste buds recovered within weeks after the chemotherapy stopped. There was so much thrown at this body by the cancer cells, poison of chemotherapy along with butchering of so many body parts, the body's ability to heal, persevere, and keep the life going was miraculous to observe. We are so fragile as human bodies, yet so strong! Even now, joint aches and mouth breakouts happen when I am under physical or mental stress. I have learnt to deal with these outbreaks through yoga, meditation, and medication. The teeth took a beating too during chemo. These require a lot more care due to setting in of periodontal disease.

Two months later, surgery for breast reconstruction took place. The surgeon even gave tattoos for the nipples which put a radiant smile on my face. Out of all the surgeries, this was the easiest to recover from. I started working from home within days. Over time, I was glad that I got the reconstruction surgery done as I didn't have to deal with putting in pads in the bra as I was planning on.

The infusion port was removed four weeks later when the blood test indicated that the cancer was in remission. This was an easy recovery as the port was right below the skin above the left breast. The port was extremely useful during the chemotherapy infusion as the nurses did not have to struggle with finding my little blood vessels. The blood vessels on my right arm were already bruised quite badly from bi-weekly blood draws for testing before every chemo infusion. I could not use my left arm for blood draw because the lymph nodes had been removed from the left armpit during earlier surgery for tumor abscission. As useful as the infusion port was, I really disliked having it in my body. I never touched it even while bathing to apply soap. Over many weeks after the port was inserted, dead skin formed a dark layer on top of the port which worried the physicians as they were concerned if it was some sort of fungus growth. The skin test revealed that it was not anything serious which put everyone's mind at ease.

Kiran Joshi, Ph.D.

Another development after the reconstruction surgery was the spread of one birthmark under my left foot. That birthmark used to be a small dark dot for as long as I could remember; one day, I noticed that it had spread into a splotch, the size of a penny with jagged edges. This area was removed with minor surgery and the cells were tested which confirmed that the spread was non-cancerous. I do not remember much pain from this surgery although I could not put any weight on my foot for about a week. When my family found out about this, they were quite concerned as my sister-in-law, who was a nurse, commented from the place of love, "Where and when is it going to end?" This all seemed quite minor to me, and I do not recall being worried about it. The birthmark has come back over the years. It is at the same spot and looks like a black spec of sand.

During every surgery, there were a couple of positive aspects if you want to call them that. One was the hot air that would warm up my cold body inside the hospital gown before the surgery, and the second was the anesthesia. With the latter, I was there and then I just dozed off to wake up rested and renewed. Then the anesthesia would wear off and the excruciating pain would take over. But it felt like life had been reset with a fresh start after waking up from the anesthesia.

Faith and Perseverance – My Journey

Within weeks, I returned to work and started exercising at the gym and the routine was established of "normal" life. I still stared at my chest in the mirror every time I changed. The two long scars from the armpit to the middle of each reconstructed breast were forbidding; these are still there but I pay less attention to them now that many years have passed. For the first five years or so, the memory of certain dates such as the day I first felt the lump would haunt me. I made the decision after five years or so that this was all in the past and I had to move on. Cancer is not something that I am controlled by anymore.

People around me called me "brave" for managing the whole situation "so well." It did not feel heroic to me – this illness had knocked at my door, and I did my best to deal with it. Over the years, I have continued to feel stronger both physically and mentally. Returning to an exercise routine even more vigorously has been beneficial. A meditation practice where I can clearly see that everything, including my body, is temporary has helped mentally. I have also realized that certain physical conditions transpired the breast cancer showing up in my body. This has been freeing.

The preciousness and precariousness of life stays with me from the place of astonishment that I am still alive. On top of that, having a vigorous and wholesome day in this life is such a blessing when I can step out for a walk with enough robustness, go to the gym or work, and eat whatever I want. I have a profound gratefulness for this brief life.

During this time, I grew spiritually. One book that I read during this time was "The Wise Heart" by Jack Kornfield as I mentioned above, which opened the doors to more Buddhist books during this time as I wrote above. I will describe my spiritual journey in detail later in the book. Another positive aspect of this time was that I became more open with friends. Although no one told me this, I knew that I was reserved with people mostly because I was very much focused on portraying a certain image which included achievements and perfection. Unknowingly, I had created a certain persona of myself to others that I was protecting by not allowing them to get to know the real me. Some of this likely made me appear reserved or unfriendly to others, as I realized during the treatments. During my younger years, one person commented that I walked and talked as if I was heading on a mission. In the past few years, many of these behaviors have changed as I have learned to be present and really listen along with contributing to whatever it is. I am still achieving in my professional life, but I also enjoy the journey of fellow human beings while doing so. Life overall has become more pleasant as I have dropped my guard to some extent.

As I have reflected on the entire situation, I cannot help but think about what decisions I would make if the cancer came out of remission. Sometimes I feel that if there is a next time, it would be time for this disease to take me if it wants. I have no fear of death as it is not annihilation as believed in Hinduism and Buddhism.

As with every life, I have had my experience of joys and sorrows. Life has offered so much; there are few worldly events left that would be different compared to what I have already experienced. My children are older now. They have become wonderful, independent individuals who are contributing positively to society. They will be fine in life without me.

I do passionately believe that we are not an accident in this Universe, where we are obliterated once the body dies. The consciousness or soul is not annihilated when we die; after death of this body, the soul goes "home" to where that source is. The soul is reincarnated until we have reached the purity of "Godhood" which will eventually lead to immortality. For now, I will be back in some form of life to deal with the consequences

Kiran Joshi, Ph.D.

of karma in this life and previous lives. Then again, who really knows what this Universal Mystery of birth and death is?

Kiran Joshi, Ph.D.

3. CALL TO DESTINY

The call to spiritual life came at an early age for me. As a five-year-old, I relocated from New Delhi, the capital of India, to the small town of Phillaur in the Northern Indian province of Punjab (Map 1). My father was immigrating to Canada in 1969, and we (my mother, two brothers, and I) were to live in Phillaur with our grandparents and other extended family members until we departed to join him. It was quite common at that time for men to immigrate alone so that they could earn enough money to invite the rest of the family.

Our house was right next to a temple dedicated to the Hindu Lion Goddess. The temple had a huge peepal (Ficus Religiosa) tree that leaned on to our house terrace; it was so ancient that I admired its massive base and beautiful fluttering leaves. There were prayers at the temple daily and kirtan (devotional singing) every Tuesday evening.

I had more of an inward personality. Instead of playing with the children after school, I used to run over to the temple to join the kirtan or just visit for a few minutes. That is where I was happy; no one else from my family went to these prayers or kirtan as my family was not religious. I do not consider myself religious, but I was fascinated by the Goddess's powerful statue – peaceful face, mounted on a lion, weapons in hand, and an evil figure under the lion's foot. It thrilled me that a female God was so mighty and serene at the same time. There was a lamp lit up along with incense in the inner sanctum of the temple. When I was little, I did not know what the symbols on the Goddess meant. I was just enchanted by her prominence and with the peace this place furnished me.

Over the years, I learnt that in the Goddess statue, the lion symbolized courage while the weaponry represented discrimination in action and righteousness, along with detachment. The evil under her lion's foot was symbolic of destroying our inner unacceptable tendencies. The flame at the temple was meant for destroying the attendees' inner darkness, while smoke from the incense was meant for purification of the space. I loved ringing the bell hanging from the ceiling when I went; I was so little that to reach the bell, I would make a running start and jump to it. The bell was meant to bring the attendees' attention to the present moment. I think of that temple even now although I have not seen it for over 40 years. I wonder if it still stands as I remember it, or if it has been renovated, or if it has been demolished to construct something else on the site!

Kiran Joshi, Ph.D.

When we first arrived in Phillaur, my older brother and I were placed in this home school nearby that was run by an old woman and her daughter. I learnt the price that one might pay for telling the truth in this school. We had been given some writing homework. The next day, when the old lady checked the work, she asked me who did the assignment. I told her that I did. She simply did not believe that a kindergartner could have such penmanship. She started hitting me with a stick ordering me to submit that my older brother did my homework. I simply would not tell her what she wanted to hear while she kept hitting me. It was, in fact, quite traumatic. I came home in tears, and my kind mother moved us to a proper private school, and that was where we studied for many years. This incident stayed with me over the years because it was the first and the only time someone used force to try to get me to admit to something that was not true. Even at the age of five, I would not do it. Truthfulness has been important to me although I did slip from time to time when I was younger. Being truthful is a strong pillar of speech that I rarely slip from anymore. I fully acknowledge that this example is nothing compared to the intense torture many people have gone through because they would not submit to what someone else wanted them to say!

There was one block in between our house and the start of the colony of the untouchable community. Although these people cleaned our latrines, I wondered how they lived when they were done hauling human waste on their heads. There was an opportunity to visit one of their homes; I do not remember why. Their dwellings were poor, but inside was like any other household, although with fewer material things. I clearly remember seeing a rudimentary cooking area in one corner with utensils and buckets. The floors were made of dirt. There was little furniture except some jute cots lined up against the walls. Clothes were hung on a string. Despite their limited possessions, these people seemed happy. Everyone appeared bathed and clean after their day's work was done.

Beyond the untouchable community was the colony of leather tanners who were also considered untouchables. I also wondered what their life was like. Looking closer on one visit, it was not any different inside their homes. The homes were poor dwellings; inside, the lives were the same as described for the untouchable community above.

While learning about Gandhi, I was deeply touched by how he treated the untouchables. His philosophy that no human being is any less than the other really appealed to me. The same message

Kiran Joshi, Ph.D.

resonated with me in the book by Tracy Kidder on Paul Farmer's life titled, "Mountains Beyond Mountains." He noted that the problem with our world is that we think that some lives matter less than other lives. These are powerful life lessons which stay with me while I work on seeing the "sameness" in all.

My grandparents lived in a village nearby. Although there were municipal buses and rickshaws one could take to visit them, going to that village on a horse cart called a "tonga" was my favorite activity. The "clop, clop" sound of the hoofbeat on the thoroughfare and the slow movement of the tonga by the green fields and ponds remain beautiful memories. My grandmother cooked in a primitive kitchen using buffalo dung patties that she made herself or the chopped wood from the farm trees. The house was made of bricks and had a water well for cooking and irrigating the fields nearby. Often, she cooked food for the workers at the farm. I would notice that the rotis (homemade flat bread) made for the workers were thicker and bigger compared to the ones she made for the family. When I inquired, her response was that since they were manual laborers, they needed more food to quench their appetite!

Faith and Perseverance – My Journey

Separated but next to the house was a paddock where a few buffaloes were kept. There were also servant's quarters in that area. In the evenings, most day workers would leave the farm while one main farmhand and his family stayed in a meager space close to the buffalo shed. When done with his work in the fields each day, the man sat with loose boxer shorts and no shirt on a rope cot while smoking a hookah. The hookah smelled different than the smoke from my grandfather's cigarettes. Over time, I learnt from the family members that his hookah likely had wild marijuana. His toddler children ran around naked from the waist down. Around the kids' waist would be knitted black string with tiny bells; when they moved, the jingles from their bells would be in the air. The wife was always pleasant when talking to my grandparents. These were happy people even though they had so little.

There was one simple, yet well-lit room attached to my grandparents' house where they kept harvest of grain or rice from their own fields before sale and for the family's use. There were plenty of traps in the space to catch the mice who came to feast on the crops. There was also a barn where the animal feed was kept. Rice husk was mixed with freshly cut green alfalfa or something similar to make the feed. The animals were bathed twice a day before milking and given feed and water twice a day. The most exciting part of being close to these animals was when the moms would give birth to baby calves. Although I never actually was allowed to witness the birthing process, it was amusing to watch the baby on its four legs the same day, running around its mama in such an uncoordinated fashion. For several weeks after the birth, the baby would drink the milk from its mother for as long as it wanted each day before my grandparents would milk it. Watching all this was delightful.

My grandfather used the male buffaloes to plow the fields for a while; over time, he bought a tractor and modern machinery. My grandparents grew wheat, corn, rice, potatoes, sugarcane, fruits, and vegetables. The farm was only ten acres or so, but it appeared grand to me. White and pink guavas, sugarcane, and fresh corn were my favorites. My grandparents milked the buffaloes a couple of times a day and sent the fresh milk, butter, yogurt, and buttermilk along with fruits and vegetables to our extended family in the town nearby daily. It was my uncle or older brother's job to bicycle to the farm every morning to fetch these items.

The best furniture at the farm was my grandmother's ornate almirah that her family had given her as a dowry. It had elegant designs carved into the wood, and the knobs were attractively made of ivory and brass with intricate designs. I adored its beauty.

My grandmother preferred her grandsons when it came to showing love. This was evident to me even at a young age. While making flat breads, she would make sure that the boys' bread was more enriched with butter compared to what she made for the rest of the family. She would be in so much emotional pain if I ever beat up my brother; she would comment that he needed to eat more so that he could fight a girl and win. All this makes me laugh as I think of it now. My grandfather adored me though. He would ask me loudly to do mental math calculations and spell difficult English words in front of others as he tried to display my smartness. Once when we were travelling on a city bus, he asked me to spell the word "bridge" as the bus crossed a river. I kept saying "bridg." He was not pleased as he stared at me with his signature angry glance where his face would contort with bulged eyes. Then, he quietly corrected me.

My grandparents worked hard, and I cherished my time with them at the farm. Their work ethic must have affected my young mind as toiling is all I know.

Kiran Joshi, Ph.D.

My grandfather, in fact, was a teacher by profession in India. His sister married a man in British Columbia, Canada, and she invited my grandfather to join them in the 1960's. He settled in northern British Columbia in the town of Wells, close to Quesnel, and about 750 km north of Vancouver (Map 2). He, then, invited his sons to Canada over the years. When my grandfather was in Canada, his asthma became worse over time due to his smoking habit. The frigid winters of Canada contributed to his asthma making it difficult for him to continue to live in Canada. After five years or so, he returned to Punjab, India, to buy a farm of his own.

He was loving yet a disciplinarian as he did not tolerate laziness from any family member or a hired hand. His sharp glance was enough to convey that one better get moving with the assigned task. In addition to operating the farm, he also made herbal medicines. To me, all his medicines looked the same – little black balls which might as well have been some animal droppings. I do not know what he used in making those medicines. However, I do remember that random people would drop by to see him and get his medicines. They showed him utter reverence when they arrived by giving him a big smile and touching his feet for blessings. My grandmother gave them something nourishing such as buttermilk or tea to drink while they chatted with my grandfather. I never saw anyone paying for the medicines. From time to time, I would understand from the discussion among the family members that these were his former students. To my young eyes, they all looked old.

My favorite part of visiting the farm was running barefoot on the fresh-dewed green grass in the mornings on the edge of the fields. The chill would rise from the bottom of my feet through my body to my head, which was heavenly. Next to that experience was sleeping outside and staring at the stars while lying in a cot at night. My grandma's cooking was quite delicious too, as she would cook lentils, beans, vegetables, and rice kheer in a seasoned clay pot on low heat that was buried in the glowing embers after the flames in the rudimentary clay oven (called choohlah) had died down. The comforting aroma of the slow cooking dish mixed with the light smoky wood-burning smell permeated the air which made me hungry. I could not wait for the food to be served.

At night, my grandfather listened to the wholesale prices of crops on his little transistor radio followed by Punjabi folk songs. I remember some of the songs – some that invited loving banter between my grandparents which I did not comprehend at that age. I realized this many years later that they were flirting with each other while listening to these songs. The lifestyle at the farm was peaceful unless my grandparents were arguing with each other or with the workers. These moments did not affect me in any negative way that I recall. As a part of the farm scene, I can't forget two or three guard dogs who were free to roam the farm and the surrounding areas. At mealtimes, they were always back where they would get roti and buttermilk.

Often, my mom, brothers, and cousins were with me at the farm. We would play in the water that was flowing through the channels for irrigating the fields while pretending to be swimming. On hot days, the mourning doves would coo early in the morning, and my grandfather would predict how hot the day was going to be by listening to their sounds.

In the town where we lived, I walked to school with my cousins. The high school was a government-run school, and it was nothing fancy in terms of the building structures. Some of our classes were even held outside under the shade of a tree where the teacher had a chair and the rest of us sat on the matted dirt floor. The teachers were kind and enthusiastic, and taught us math, English, local and national languages, along with the sciences, world history and geography. I had eagerness for learning from an early age. During summer holidays between all school years, we got the books for the next school year. Over the summertime, I would finish reading science, literature, and history books.

The story books on heroes such as Bhagat Singh or Jhansi ki Rani who fought the British Raj enchanted me. There was ample teaching from Ramayana and Mahabharata (ancient Indian epics) all around us from stories being told in families or in the neighborhood. Ramayana, the story of good over evil, got enacted in open air theaters of city streets around the festival of Diwali every fall season. Although I do not remember the story of Mahabharata being enacted in the streets, the story is about taking right action to destroy evil. The valor that the heroes displayed in these epics was beyond commendable and impressionable on my developing mind. I wanted to be just like the heroes in these stories. As I re-read these epics over the years, I also realized that they were humans with their own follies to contend with.

Outside the school boundary, there were beggars with leprosy sitting on jute mats looking miserable, dark, and dirty. Many were missing fingers or toes. Often, their noses were distorted. I gave them money routinely from my small daily allowance. Their plight in that physical body used to touch me deeply. I pondered whether they had children, or where they lived! I never got those answers when I lived in India. My later research showed me that this disease is controllable with antibiotics if caught early, and it is not as contagious as thought before when people with leprosy were shunned. There still are more than a quarter-million people in the world with this disease. Before my life is over, I intend to volunteer at a leprosy center in India.

My dad's sister was a math teacher at our school. She took immense pride in the fact that I was the top student in the class. In addition to my mom, I had a lot of help from her in my studies. My dad's brother, who was an avid reader, also supported my studies. When we left for Canada, he gave me two books that I still own – one was "My Experiments with Truth" by Mahatma Gandhi, and the second was "Bhagavad Geeta (The Song of Lord, Ancient Indian Scripture)" by Radhakrishnan. I treasure these books, not because these were the first two books someone gifted me, but due to the impression their repetitive readings have had on me.

"My Experiments with Truth," Gandhi's autobiography from his childhood to 1921, explored his principles of nonviolence and truth while living the spiritual and physical dimensions of his life. This book impresses upon me that truthfulness can be a formidable guiding force in life, no matter what the situation is. And that life is a series of experiments; as long as we learn from each experiment, we are successful. If there is no learning from a situation, the experiment is a failure.

The main question that the Bhagavad Geeta addressed was how to proceed morally and ethically when confronted with decision, and whether it was right to act or not in a difficult situation. Bhagavad Geeta is, in fact, an episode in Mahabharata that was mentioned above. This book is a treasure-trove for spiritual seekers. One can open any page in it and read just that page, and one is guaranteed to find spiritual nuggets. From repeated study of this book, what impressed upon me deeply is that it is only the body that dies while the soul cannot be annihilated. The soul is reborn in another body until nirvana is reached.

These family members made me successful by encouraging me to explore my full potential, and I could not be more indebted. Unfortunately, my aunt died at the age of 32 from unknown causes. I miss her dearly. She and my father had a close bond, as she was the youngest and the only girl out of the five siblings and my father the oldest. Even when women hardly completed high school, my grandfather and my dad supported her ambition to get a bachelor's degree in mathematics while staying in a

Kiran Joshi, Ph.D.

hostel away from home. What were these liberal men thinking, I wonder? Without saying a word, were they ensuring that her future was secure regardless of the presence of a husband in her life?

My aunt was married to a man who had a weak physical constitution but was quite an intellect. He had a Ph.D. in geography. I looked up to him, and he was definitely the inspiration behind me also doing a Ph.D. degree, although in chemistry.

Growing up, we used to sleep on the terrace on warm nights. I loved contemplating the stars in the sky at nighttime. At the age of nine or ten, I used to think about what existed beyond this universe. It made me feel very pressed down and uneasy. One prayer I remember chanting quietly in bed every night was, "May all beings be happy, may all beings be safe." I must have picked it up from my mother at an early age because even now, I hear her chanting something like this throughout the day. I have been blessed with pious and progressive parents who put their children's welfare and education before themselves always. At the same time, they had expectations from us that we would stay out of trouble and focus on our studies.

Faith and Perseverance - My Journey

My dad was in civil engineering-related projects in New Delhi. He, in fact, held an excellent job as a senior draftsman with the Central Government of India for building hydroelectric dams. When he came to Canada, he worked in a lumber mill to earn his living, since the Canadian government did not recognize his engineering credentials from India. He described to me that the first night after work at the mill, he cried the whole night. It took him a year to become comfortable with doing the manual work in the lumber mill. Since his brothers were in Quesnel, he settled there too.

So far north in Quesnel, the winters were unbelievably frigid with negative 40-degree temperatures, and the lumber mills at that time were open on the sides. He worked different shifts week to week and carried a grey plastic lunch kit when he left home. When he returned, he looked disheveled and had a distinct smell of fresh wood on his clothing. If I were at home, I would run out to take his lunch kit from him. When people asked what he did, he called himself a "stripper" because his job was to pick up the wood strips that had fallen on the ground from the machinery while being sawed. I thought of his title amusingly! After taking a shower, he would sit down for a hot meal and end his day with vanilla ice cream topped with canned fruit cocktail. His weekend routine included grocery shopping at

Kiran Joshi, Ph.D.

many stores based on the sale at the time, along with a visit to "Popshop" (a soda store) across Quesnel River (Map 2) which flowed so beautifully through the town. This river starts at Quesnel Lake in the town of Likely (150 km away from Quesnel) and is a major tributary to Fraser River, the longest river in British Columbia, which starts in the Canadian Rockies (Map 2). The city has done an amazing job of building a paved riverfront trail loop through the neighborhoods, which is beautifully lined with hanging flower baskets in the summertime.

Once, when I was helping him unload the groceries, I dropped and broke a whole case of beer. While I was frightened, looking at the mess, there were no harsh words from him. Instead, he said, "Let us clean up. No use crying over spilled milk."

My father was kind and gentle with us except for a few outbursts with one of my siblings. He cried when he got the news that his beloved sister had passed away unexpectedly. Her passing saddened me very much too since she was so instrumental in my educational success in India.

My father had self-learnt palmistry. He stopped making any predictions from this art after someone showed him his palm, and he was not able to tell him that he was going to die soon. He also knew about me falling seriously ill in my 40's, but he never told me until afterwards. When he found out about my cancer, he told me afterwards that he knew that I would survive it.

Although I was aloof as a child, my childhood in Phillaur overall was carefree. In addition to kirtan at the Lion Goddess temple, I was always interested in cleaning the house. Cleaning is something that I keep coming back to even now, especially on difficult days. I find it gives me peace by cleansing the thoughts in my mind. A saint that I will talk about later has appeared in my dreams sweeping in front of my forehead. This symbol has stayed with me - a holy man was trying to get me initiated in spirituality by removing the mess from my mind! Walking in nature, tending to plants, and pulling weeds are also activities that I enjoyed doing from childhood. While weeding, I remind myself I have to pull out the roots or the weeds will resurface. This also grounds me that unless I pull out the roots of my bad habits, they will resurface.

4. BECOMING NOBODY

Eleven years after my dad arrived in Canada, we too came to Quesnel (Map 2). During these years, he visited us three times in India, six months to one year at a time. Although we would have preferred to spend our younger years with him, we were well taken care of by our extended family.

My mom, brothers, and I flew from New Delhi to Vancouver on Japan Airlines with an overnight stay near the Narita Airport. It was our first adventure being on an airplane and stepping outside India. We were excited. Noodles were served on the plane, which I enjoyed thoroughly compared to the rest of the family. I ended up eating some of their portions as well as they did not like the smooth and slippery texture. From an early age, I was open to trying new foods which served me well in my life as I now make and enjoy vegetarian foods from many different ethnicities. There was a fuel stop in Bangkok, Thailand, where we got off the plane for a couple of hours on the way to the Narita airport. I had never felt such stifling heat before in the dry plains of Punjab, far away from large water bodies. Next, we landed in Japan. The airline placed us in a hotel room overnight since we had to wait for the next connecting flight to Vancouver. My brothers and I decided to explore the areas outside the hotel on foot. We came to a pedestrian cross walk. Within seconds, all traffic stopped to allow us to cross to the other side. We were oblivious to what was going on, and it took a few seconds to register that these vehicles had stopped for us! This is a good laugh even now when I look back because it is different than what happens in India where one must fight the honking traffic and stray animals on congested roads in order to cross.

My father was at the Vancouver airport to pick us up. It was marvelous to see him. I do not remember the thoughts running through my head as we rode in a taxi to the Greyhound bus station to catch the overnight bus to Quesnel except that we were joyous. There was certainly a sense of everything being different, including the pastries that he bought at the bus station café. None of us ate much because these just did not taste good. Our father packed them up to take them with us on the bus.

My mom was wearing an elegant sari of red and grey colors with lovely designs in it; all of a sudden in my eyes, she did not fit in as everyone else around her was in Western outfit. I am not quite sure what her feelings were about this, but fairly soon

Kiran Joshi, Ph.D.

after we arrived, she started wearing blouses and pants. She had brought a couple of her favorite quilts along with other luggage when we travelled to Canada; suddenly, that bundle of quilts, although properly packaged and neatly placed on the bus platform before loading, looked out of place to me. I do not remember how I felt about these observations, but I was aware that we were in a different country.

We arrived in Quesnel early in the morning. Our uncle, my dad's brother, drove us from the bus station to my dad's little house in Quesnel in his red station wagon. It could not have been more than seven hundred square feet of space, but we were blissful. It was clean, had running hot water, and shaggy green carpets. Since it was already September, the chill of the autumn season was setting in, and the small front yard was full of falling leaves from the massive willow tree that grew there. The backyard had grass and a white picket fence. It held a small rickety wooden bench which became my favorite spot to sun in while studying. There was a big window in the dining room overlooking the backyard which also became my domain as I studied and watched the snowfall during the winter.

Within a week, my dad and uncle took my brothers and me to our respective schools to get us registered, and I was admitted to

12th grade. Getting adjusted to the new school in Quesnel, culture, and spoken language took time. From being a top student in India, I found myself as nobody in the Canadian school system. Since I joined the school a couple of weeks after it started, the seats in the classrooms were taken and I got relegated to the last seat in everyone.

The first few glimpses of racism came early after I arrived in Canada, which stay with me even after all these years. At the school, my locker was next to that of a Caucasian girl who was well-proportioned in size compared to me. The first few weeks when we would both be using the lockers at the same time, she would constantly elbow the left side of my ribs giving me quite a few bruises. Although her bullying made me angry, I had to ignore it as my English was not good enough to say anything to her. This went on for several weeks until she must have realized that she was not going to get any reaction out of me. She stopped eventually but maintained that snarl of disgust on her face whenever she saw me in the hallways. Her behavior deeply saddened me.

Racism took place outside of school as well. My aunt took three of her children and me to a local drug store. We were wandering around the store while she finished her shopping. I noticed that someone was closely following us gaggle of kids. I did not think much of it until we stepped outside the store. The woman who was closely following us in the store came running out and asked me if I had taken something from the store without paying. I told her that I had not. She ordered me to empty my purse. She found nothing of course. There were no apologies; she just left. Were you following us because you saw some brown kids wandering around the store? I will never know.

Although I write of these moments, there was a lot of kindness too. The Jehovah's Witness folks would come by on Sundays with their small booklets. It was a good opportunity to practice my English skills. At the school, it was not the Indian students who tried to befriend me; instead, it was Caucasian students who were helpful, especially the boys in my physics class. For some reason, the Indian girls in my classes were neutral towards me while a couple of Caucasian girls who enjoyed Indian food started walking home with me. Although I was grateful for this companionship, I was all right with not having any close friends. My focus was very much on advancing my verbal skills and excelling in my classes.

It took a while to get used to some students being disrespectful to the teachers in the classrooms. This was vastly different from the culture of regard towards teachers, elders, and authorities from which I had come. In the beginning, watching the outbursts from the students towards the teachers used to stress me out as they were yelling at me. Over time, the impact lessened.

Mathematics was quite straightforward as I had mastered harder concepts in India. During the first math test, I did not even own a calculator and had done all computations on paper. The teacher was quite agitated with the class for low grades and ordered us to show up an hour early the next morning. Not knowing that this message was not for me, I appeared early the next day. He looked at me with a big smile on his face and said, "You did not need to be here since you aced the exam." It made me joyful, but I never really felt like I was doing especially well given the language barrier and the cultural differences to get through.

In the beginning, I used to meet a few times a week with an "English as a Second Language (ESL)" teacher. Within a few weeks, she told me that I did not need to see her anymore because I had progressed quickly. In English class, we were reading "One Flew Over the Cuckoo's Nest" by Ken Kesey. We also watched the movie of the same title in class. Our assignment was to draft a comparative essay; I had not heard of such assignments before. I do not think that I understood the novel or the movie at that time. The only thing that I noted was that Jack Nicholson's acting was very strange. This was the first English novel I had read and the first English movie I had watched. I do not remember how I did on the assignment, but I passed the class somehow. In geometry class, there was a discussion around "curling." I was thinking about the curls in the hair; how did the word "broom" fit in the same conversation? This all sounds so comical now.

As Grade 12 progressed, I started noticing someone who looked pregnant. One day in one of the classes, the teacher asked what we planned to do after we graduated from high school. The female student and her boyfriend announced that they were getting married and having a baby. While the entire class rejoiced at their announcement, this was quite shocking to me as they were so young. Becoming pregnant before getting married was a new concept for me. It was not that pregnancies outside marriage did not happen in India; this just was not something that I had been exposed to before.

The physics teacher in Grade 12 was kind and helped me a lot. The students in the class who were all male except for one also helped me. This teacher took our class to visit the universities in the Greater Vancouver area. A family of a physician and a nurse whose son was from a local school hosted both us girls. It was the first time I had the experience of living in a Caucasian family's home. They were a welcoming and hospitable family who made sure that there were nuts on the dinner table for me as a protein source. We had dinner together the first night we got there. The next morning when I came down to the kitchen, both parents were gone, and their son offered cereal for breakfast. It was surprising to not see the mother there as my mom was always present when we came to the kitchen!

While we were visiting the universities in Vancouver, I was wearing cheap brown foam-top shoes which provided no protection from water. It rained when we were there as it normally does in Vancouver for many months. During the visit, my shoes were totally soaked; the hosts had a white carpet. When we returned, I was conflicted on how to not get their carpet dirty and how to dry my shoes. I removed the shoes and socks before stepping inside the house, and then placed them on the electric heater in the guest bathroom to dry. Another student who was rooming with me was totally astonished when she saw the shoes on the heater; she came out of the bathroom and asked

Kiran Joshi, Ph.D.

what I was doing. It was clear that she had not confronted such issues!

Our hosts' house in Vancouver was luxurious. When we returned from the trip, I was so excited to tell my family about them and the house. I mentioned to my dad that one day, I would own a house like that. He had a gentle smile on his face and stated that anything was possible if I worked hard. This has remained the theme from him towards me throughout our lives.

Although we visited three different universities (UBC, SFU, and BCIT) in Vancouver and the surrounding area, I fell in love with the University of British Columbia (UBC) from the first sight. I did my first year of higher education at a college in the nearby town of Prince George upon the suggestion of the high school counselor and transferred to UBC from the second year on. My mother and younger brother stayed with me in the college town during the first year, which was a two-hour drive from Quesnel. We rented a basement suite from a warm family. I took a bus every day to college as there was no money to buy another car; neither did I have the driver's license at that time. Taking the bus in the non-winter months was not a problem, but not during the high winter months when the temperatures often dipped to - 40 degrees. One day, I kept waiting for the bus to arrive in biting, freezing weather while returning from the college until I simply could not feel my hands. I ran inside the college building and called my mother to ask what to do. That was one time she gave me permission to take a cab home.

My father visited us on the weekends. Due to the extremely frigid winter, the blood vessels in his nose would crack and he would bleed so much that I was frightened. I will never be able to repay all the sacrifices that my parents made to send me to college. Money was tight in our family, but my father made sure that I had no education debt. For many years, we wore clothes and shoes bought from stores such as K-Mart and Saan Stores. Purchasing items from Zellers, Hudson Bay, and Eaton's came years later. The fact remained, though, that we had a clean home, loving parents, plenty to eat, and clean clothes on our backs. There was access to medical doctors and dentists. The schooling was paid for by my parents. What more could one ask for?

From the second year of college, I transferred to UBC to begin higher education in chemistry. It didn't even occur to me that I should apply at other universities in addition to UBC in case I was rejected. Chemistry came naturally although it still required studying. Living in the dorms among the English-speaking community helped me excel in verbal skills.

To graduate with the bachelor's degree at UBC, everyone had to pass a standardized English writing exam before the last semester of senior year. It had a low passing rate at the first try even for the native English speakers. I failed this exam the first two tries. The second time I failed it, I was furious with myself. With tears flowing, I walked from the building where the results were posted directly to the English department across campus to understand what led to this catastrophe! I clearly recall some students staring at my tear-stained face as they passed by me. The administrator showed me the errors and pointed me to a writing class on the weekends which might help. Of course, I was attentive and enrolled immediately. This allowed me to pass the writing exam with flying colors on the next attempt. I remember being so elated when the transcript arrived at home that I did a somersault in my parents' living room. I never felt such jubilation at any other grade as I did with this one. For this essay, my transcript showed "*C*" for "*Completed.*" My parents could simply not understand that a "*C*" on my transcript made me so joyful until I explained it to them. In hindsight, this failure taught me to write better; it took me one step closer to authoring this book.

Although I was getting good grades in my classes, I did not have a sense of my achievements until I applied for a summer internship at the Canadian Nuclear Laboratories in Pinawa, Manitoba. I learned of the posting from a flyer in the student resource center. It was thrilling when I got the internship since it paid $20 an hour and was related to chemistry. I called my parents to let them know. My father surveyed the map and told me that he could not find this town, but he still helped me figure out how to get there via Winnipeg, Manitoba. There, my manager commented one day that these internships were merit based and were given to students country-wide who had done well in their studies. He used the term "cream of the crop" to describe the interns. My manager and the scientists in the lab were extremely kind and helpful. I got my first publication in a scientific journal from this research.

All the students stayed in dormitory-style housing and a bus drove us back and forth to the worksite. We all worked hard during weekdays. On the weekends, drinking hard liquor was common among the interns. This was not appealing to me at all. Smoking among the interns was also common which ended up giving me severe eye and skin allergies. These were smart people and I fit in fine except for partying. There was a lake near the dormitories where the students swam during free time. I

Kiran Joshi, Ph.D.

took it upon myself to take swimming lessons at the Pinawa community pool so that I could swim with them. It was thrilling to learn this skill.

One of my co-workers there was adamant about me meeting one of her male friends from a nearby town. When this nice man drove up to pick me up, I had a female friend in tow ready to go with us. He was polite when we were together but we did not meet again. The female friend wanted to watch a "country" movie, and that is what we did. She mentioned afterwards that he wanted to be alone with me. I was naïve and did not have the concept of dating or a boyfriend at that time.

After returning to UBC, I started getting small scholarships without applying. I must have been doing well without realizing! I graduated with Honors and applied to graduate school in chemistry at UBC and the University of Toronto. I was accepted at both. I chose to study at UBC since it was closer to home. I ended up with an amiable group of people and a professor to do my research where I went on to complete my Ph.D. with "first" class standing in the thesis. It was becoming more obvious that there were not that many women as I progressed further into chemistry at UBC. There were only two females including me among the group of many male researchers in the graduate school lab. This trend continued to some extent that I will talk more about later.

During graduate school, my research project yielded results quickly as I was done with my master's and Ph.D. in five years total. Blood and tears were poured into achieving the results. The weekdays were long with research, classes, and the teaching assistant duties.

I must have been quite self-centered around my achievements during this time, though. In our lab, we had some common responsibilities around tasks such as changing gas cylinders or transporting commonly used chemicals. One day, one of my colleagues commented that the person with the most results did the smallest number of common tasks. Since I was sensitive by nature, these comments hit me like a brick. I used to do these tasks, but evidently less often than others! From that day on, I became more in tune with what was expected of me and did not allow anyone to make such remarks ever again.

Although all the graduate students and the postdoctoral fellows in my lab were hard working, there was one Ph.D. student who used to compete with others to get the most prime time for certain instrument use. The Nuclear Magnetic Resonance

Kiran Joshi, Ph.D.

Imaging machines, which were incredibly useful to decipher our work, were in high demand. The sign-up sheet for blocking the time slot to use these machines during the upcoming week would get filled up within minutes of it being mounted on the board. We used to line up a few minutes ahead of when the sheet would be posted. Once, he inquired when I intended to line up for the sign-up sheet. I did not think much of it and told him. When I arrived, he was already sitting there ahead of me. This was quite hilarious; we both looked at each other and smiled, acknowledging what had just happened. Once done, we walked back to the lab. And the same day, I accidentally broke his glassware which was in short supply. He was livid but got over it quickly. These two incidents happening the same day still makes me gleeful.

The Ph.D. thesis writing turned out to be an excellent opportunity to hone my writing skills further. One of my advisors who reviewed the first draft was a British professor who was an absolute stickler when it came to writing style. On top of that, he had a dry sense of humor that I often did not understand. I dropped the first few chapters for him to assess which came back with plenty of red markings. I learnt quickly from him, however, and got on with revising and writing the rest of the chapters. Finally, the last chapter came back from him with no corrections and a flattering "Well done." Now, that was heartening. The perseverance including being open to feedback and correcting the course as needed was paying off.

I completed the Ph.D. thesis oral defense with some UBC faculty members that I knew and one professor from an external university unknown to me. I obtained "First" class, and I was in heaven because it was not common to get such a grade in a Ph.D. thesis.

These were cheerful times in graduate school. We had so little financially but we were rich with using our brains, developing ourselves, strengthening friendships, and anticipating the future.

One miraculous thing that happened at UBC for me was access to vegetarian food at the dorms. I was never fond of meat or eggs while I was growing up as my stomach would hurt after eating these products. From the place of care, my mother would force me to eat these as she would remind me that I needed protein to grow. Once I arrived at UBC, there was a wide and varied selection of vegetarian food. I was elated. I never looked back to eating meat again. I go through phases with eggs even now – my stomach does not hurt anymore when I eat eggs, but I find myself turned on and off from eggs.

Kiran Joshi, Ph.D.

I made some close friends at the university that I am still in touch with. One friend encouraged me to explore Vancouver and do things other than studying, which imbued me with enthusiasm. At that time, I had no concept of same-gender attraction. One day, during some discussion, she described that another woman liked girls. I blurted out that I liked girls too as it had no sexual meaning for me. She stared at me with disbelief without saying anything and then just left the room, leaving me perplexed. Over the years, I am amused when I ponder what she must have been thinking of me at that time!

As my English improved, I started reading fiction and non-fiction books for pleasure instead of reading only for schoolwork. The first book that I read for fun was called "Terms of Endearment" by Larry McMurtry. When the movie was released based on this book, it was a treat to watch. How the mother-daughter relationship strengthened as diversity hit them remains a warm memory! I have been an avid fiction and non-fiction reader since my college years. No day is complete without opening a book at my night table and reading it before I go to bed. Reading is as therapeutic as talking to a trusted friend or being in nature.

Faith and Perseverance – My Journey

I met my dear husband during my first year of graduate school at UBC. He had come to the UBC Chemistry Department from the Indian Institute of Technology (IIT), Mumbai, for higher studies three years before I joined. The Chemistry Department hosted a meet-and greet event during the first week of September 1985 for the faculty and the current graduate students to welcome the new students. This event was held at the Asian Cultural Center on the campus, next to a beautiful rose garden at the edge of Pacific Ocean. I went there with other new students. Many of us newbies sat together. As the evening progressed, at one point I looked down one of the hallways and I saw my husband walking towards our table. My first thought was, "Oh, he is cute!" I do not remember having such strong emotion about another man; so, there was some recognition. He came over and introduced himself to everyone at the table. I did not talk much with him on that day except learning his name. I left shortly after he sat down with us to attend to something else.

Over the next few weeks, we kept running into each other in the department hallways. I also noticed that he would mysteriously show up in the small chemistry department library when I was studying there. He would linger around the library bookshelves next to where I was and then slowly walk over in my direction. We made small talk.

Kiran Joshi, Ph.D.

Weeks passed. Around early December, he told me that later in the day he would be heading towards the cliffs overlooking the Pacific Ocean near the anthropology museum on the campus for some photography, and asked if I would like to join him. I did not think much of it and agreed to go. When we reached the destination, I observed that he was more interested in me being in the photos as I overlooked the ocean. I found it strange but did not say anything. We walked back to our respective places just talking. Next, he started asking me if I wanted to join him to get a coffee and UBC's infamous cinnamon bun at a nearby coffee shop where he and his friends went every morning before starting work in the lab. By this time, attraction was developing from my side too. Along came February 1986 – I was watching the movie called "An Officer and a Gentleman" with a girlfriend in my apartment when the phone rang. On the other side of the line was my husband asking me if I would like to go to the Valentine's Day dance with him. Now, that was bold! I hung up the phone after agreeing, and my girlfriend teased me, "You have a date, girl, don't you!"

On Valentine's Day, he came by my apartment with a single rose and a sentimental card. He looked dapper in his white dress shirt, grey pants, and black shoes. We went to the dance and did not spend much time together as there were a lot of common acquaintances present. He dropped me at home and left. We started going out for dinner and spending more time together over the weekends. One day at a restaurant, I caught myself pecking at his salad. I stopped when I realized that I had not done anything like that with other friends. One evening when we were together, he announced that he was trying but was having a tough time staying away from me and would like me to be his girlfriend. I melted and leaned my head on his chest. His heart was pounding loudly. When I told him that, he replied that it had not beaten like this before! There was no looking back from then. We became inseparable.

A few months went by, and my parents came to Vancouver to meet him. They liked him immensely. They used to be concerned about how they would find someone in their Punjabi community who would be equally or more educated if I were to have an arranged marriage! Thoughts of arranged marriage or not graduating with the highest degree possible with top grades never crossed my mind. My father was the most supportive as I moved from Quesnel to Vancouver for college degrees. Many of his Punjabi colleagues at the lumber mill had come from villages in India where girls did not always attend higher education. They continued this trend with their daughters in Canada too. I was the first Indian girl to go to college from

Kiran Joshi, Ph.D.

Quesnel. I was told that there was one Indian boy who had gone on to college from Quesnel before me. Most boys, both Indian and Caucasian, after Grade 12 would find good paying jobs in the local lumber and paper mills, and that is where they raised their families.

My dad's mill friends would tell him repeatedly that it was better if he married me off after Grade 12 as he may lose control of my actions once I went away for higher education. My father is of liberal mindset and openly encouraged me to follow my dreams. He used to say, "You can be anything you want." I could not have been born in a better family. Without saying a word, he likely wanted his daughter to be independent financially no matter what happened in her life. My father remains my ardent supporter and cheerleader as I go through life. Even now, when I get his greeting cards on my birthdays, he always directs these to "*DR.* Kiran Joshi." He is the only one who addresses a letter to me with that title.

I was getting paid a small stipend during graduate school while I worked as teaching assistants in the undergraduate labs. The stipend was about 12,000 Canadian dollars per year before taxes. It felt like a lot of money at that time. It was the first time in graduate school that I started taking a small plane from

Vancouver to Quesnel and back to visit my family instead of the Greyhound bus.

At the end of every school year, parents came to the campus to take their children home. I did not have that luxury as my father had to work to pay the bills. At the end of one undergraduate year, I was returning home for the summer on a Greyhound bus. I had just enough money left to buy a sandwich and pay for the bus ticket. Since I had several small bags on me, the bus driver told me that I would need to pay extra due to the number of bags. I was mortified. I had no choice but to place my first name on some bags and the last name on some other bags. The driver did not catch onto it or chose not to say anything to me.

Another financial hardship story dealt with my personal safety – I used to take the overnight bus from Quesnel to Vancouver which arrived in the city around 5 AM. Since I could not afford a cab to go to the campus from the bus depot, I would walk a few blocks to the bus stop for the municipal bus to the university campus. One day, as I stepped out of the bus depot and started walking, a car drove slowly behind me and stopped. The driver, who looked inebriated, offered to take me wherever I needed to go. My first thought was that it would be helpful if I did not have to walk to the bus stop with all these bags!

Kiran Joshi, Ph.D.

Suddenly, common sense kicked in, which prompted me to decline his offer. What would the outcome have been if I had accepted the ride? The driver left, and I decided to take a taxi from that day onwards from the bus depot to the campus. The cost was about $20, a lot of money to spend at that time. Once the graduate school stipend started coming in, it was amazing to have some financial freedom.

I continue to feel deep gratitude towards my parents for encouraging me to live my life to the highest potential and for supporting me financially when they did not have that much themselves. As my parents got older, my father asked what he should leave in his will for me. My response to him was that the gift of education was the superior gift that he had given me, and that I did not need anything more from him! He became emotional and still chose to hand me his beautifully yellow cloth-wrapped holy book, Guru Granth Sahib in Urdu, which is invaluable to me even though I cannot read Urdu. On difficult days, I pull it out of the drawer, close my eyes, and place both my hands on it. This offers me tremendous peace as I sense my father's love enveloping me.

Although my education journey started as a "Nobody" in the Canadian school system, I became "Somebody" the day I completed my Ph.D. in one of the best universities in Canada and even in the world!

Kiran Joshi, Ph.D.

5. DIVINITY IN ACTION

One of the most profound spiritual experiences during graduate school at UBC was meeting Swami Chinmayananda (respectfully also referred to as Swami Ji). He was holding Bhagavad Geeta lectures at the campus for a few days; I had not heard of him, but my husband had attended his lectures at IIT, Mumbai, before joining UBC. We started attending his lectures at the campus in the evenings.

One evening, we were running late and were the last two to walk into the lecture hall. We were darting up the stairs when I looked back after hearing some footsteps behind me. There he was – Swami Ji was right behind us with some of his handlers nearby. When I turned back, he stared directly into my eyes with a gentle smile on his face. His eyes were so full of love which penetrated me deeply. That "glance of love and mercy" from this man of God who did not even know me was so intense and unforgettable. Other than from my father, this was perhaps the first and only time when someone had looked at me with a stare that was dripping with love and no judgment. Over time, I realized that he must have been seeing me at the soul level where there was no separation between any lives. This is a central point of many spiritual disciplines that we all originate from the same source. The great seers see the same soul housed in different bodies, and it is the body that dies at the end of our life. This is the same Mahatma (great soul) that I have seen in my dream sweeping dirt from the front of my forehead.

During one of these lectures, someone placed a few dollar bills in front of him, as customary in Indian temples, when she bowed while he sat to start the lecture. That look of disgust as he directed his handlers to take the money away was impressionable. He had left all connections with the worldly things that we desire and cling to so badly. As I was growing up, my family was not religious and did not look upon Sadhus (Holy Men) as learned people, although we still offered something if a mendicant showed up at our doorstep with his begging bowl. I did not have any opinion one way or the other, but that just one momentary meeting and listening to a few of Swami Chinmayananda's talks made me peaceful and inculcated what divinity was. I learnt the meaning of "faith" at this time – Faith is to believe what we do not see. My faith was in his teachings.

Kiran Joshi, Ph.D.

Swami Chinmayananda's presence came back into my life once again when our son was born in 1997. My mother-in-law came from India to help with his rearing when he was a baby. She was aware that there was Swami Ji's mission in San Jose. We visited it a couple of times when she was with us. She was a pious woman who did her religious activities daily. After helping with our son during the first year of his life and introducing us to the Chinmaya Mission, San Jose, she went back to India.

As our daughter turned five years old, we started attending the Mission regularly; she went to the children's classes where she learned Indian mythological stories while we attended the adult gatherings where the resident teacher expounded upon Bhagavad Geeta. As our son got older, he was not that excited about having his Sundays tied up, but our daughter enjoyed both the stories from the Indian epics and time with friends. The central message of Bhagavad Geeta that stuck with me over the years is that the fruit of our actions is not up to us; only doing the action wholeheartedly is ours. Swami Chinmayananda had passed away by then; the center had teachers who had studied with him who were also learned people. They would give their own teachings along with many anecdotes from their time with Swami Ji. A few things which stayed with me over the years are:

Faith and Perseverance – My Journey

1) A teacher described that people would ask him to teach them meditation, and he would tell them that they could not learn meditation until they had a quiet mind. The reason this stuck with me was because my idea of a quiet mind at one time was "no thoughts." I would observe my thoughts and try stopping them from arising to quieten my mind. That would always fail. I realized that I could not stop the thoughts from appearing. Instead, what I had to do was to let the thoughts come and let them go instead of allowing one of them to hijack me. Now, I note the thought when it arises as "judging," "aversive," "greed," and so on. The moment I do that, the thought loses its power over me. It is also interesting to observe how my thoughts are like artificial intelligence. One type of thought keeps reappearing. It is like my mind says, this is what you thought about a few minutes ago, here it is again. When my mind gets carried away with a certain thought, I break the sequence by using the technique Jack Kornfield talks about, "Thank you for trying to keep me safe, mind. Just relax (Kornfield, Grynberg, 2023, 47:00)."[1] Constant vigilance is the key until the patterns are broken and certain habits are established which are not judgmental, greedy, or aversive.

2) One teacher touched upon that Swami Ji would tell the women to treat their husbands like God and watch the happiness

Kiran Joshi, Ph.D.

in the home increase. Of course, my immediate reactive mental response was that it was a sexist remark. Over time, I have come to understand this as treating all humans at the level of the soul which is God where everyone is the same; the commentary is less about seeing the spouse as a God; it is more about seeing Godliness in him and everyone. As I became more aware of Buddhist teachings, I came across a teaching which asked if one has looked at their partner with Buddha's eyes (or God's eyes). My husband, in fact, is God-like. His qualities are totally Satvik (virtuous or pure). There is no anger, greed, attachment, or enmity towards anyone. One will never hear him talking about anyone in a positive or a negative manner. He works hard and is grateful for whatever comes his way. I have never seen him grasp at anything; he is at peace with what is. He has made me into a better person for which I am extremely grateful.

3) Swami Ji would say there is enough money in the world to satisfy everyone, but not enough to satisfy one greedy person. As I have gotten older, I see the truth of it all around me. The disparity among rich and poor is so stark in the world. When does one say that this is enough? Or when does one think about using some of the funds to make others' lives better? How do we stop measuring our success by the yardstick of money, title, and ownership of material goods? Am I really my bank account,

my title, or my house? The more material goods one has, the more worries one has! When I see an obituary where the dead person's title is listed in front of the name, I ask myself about when someone stops playing their role of "Dr." or "CEO," for example! Are material things and my role the ones which will go with me at the end of life? While on my deathbed, what will I be thinking of? It will certainly not be the material things or my title. Although we do not know what our last moments will be like, the mind at rest and the faces of my loved ones would be the last sight I wish for. Some friends find such thoughts "morbid." I understand as they may not want to think about death! I don't dwell on death, but being aware that our time in this life is limited and of what really matters now helps us to live fully. Life is a precious gift that we must not waste. While taking an action, if we just stop and ask ourselves if that action benefits everyone, we are doing good.

4) Finally, Swami Ji would ask "how?" if anyone said, "Have a great day!" I am mindful that I want to do actions including those of speech, mind, and body which are geared towards making my day and someone else's day "great" instead of ruining it. I have extended this practice to include "seeing" people when I say, "Great to see you!" I turn towards them, look them straight in the eyes. and really "see" them when I talk to

them. I did this practice recently when I handed some money to a homeless person. I sat next to him, handed him the money, and looked in his eyes; I noted how blue and deep his eyes were. I told him that. He thanked me for "seeing" him. This made the day "great" for both of us!

Kiran Joshi, Ph.D.

6. HOW FAR WE HAVE COME?

As women, we have come far. Recently, it was heartening to see in the news that the United States government worked hard to secure the release of an African American female athlete, Brittney Griner, from a Russian prison. There are twenty or more female CEOs running Fortune 500 companies in the United States. Many countries have had female prime ministers, vice presidents, and presidents. A lot of progress has been made.

In graduate school, we were only two females in my Ph.D. research lab among a group of many male researchers. It was the same trend during the postdoctoral fellowship. Now, companies are graded on diversity and inclusion.

For me, it was during a postdoctoral position at a university in the U.S. in 1990 where I was first exposed to disturbing comments from men. An incident happened quite early on which left me perplexed; one of the two professors that I worked with said to me unexpectedly during a lunch meeting that women were like used cars - one did not know how good they were unless one drove them first. I ignored the comment as I did not know what to do with it or even give it a name; however, this meeting is engraved in my memory. Another incident involved a graduate student in the lab next door who approached me one day and asked if I was promiscuous. Let alone be promiscuous, I did not even know what the word meant! I had to look it up in the dictionary.

The time at university was quite painful as the two professors played "good cop, bad cop" with me. The bad cop constantly commented on the lack of results from my research while the good cop remained quiet. The most painful experience with the bad cop was when my 60-year-old father-in-law suddenly passed away in India due to a heart attack. Neither of the professors accepted my calls or returned my messages. I wanted to discuss taking bereavement leave for two weeks to attend his funeral and support my husband and his family. I went to India with my husband anyway after several attempts to get hold of them. The day I returned to work, the bad cop met with me in his office and told me since that it was not my father who had died, I did not need to go, and that I went for vacation. This left me speechless and extremely sad about how heartless some people could be. I walked out of his office and sat outside the good cop's lab. One of the postdoctoral fellows from the lab saw me from the window and stepped out to sit with me. He wanted to know what perturbed me. I kept silent as there were no words to explain what had just transpired. All I knew was that I wanted to get away from the bad cop's negative energy, and pledged not to be like him towards anyone when such situations arose. I suspected that the good cop was aware of what was said but chose not to do anything about it.

When the time came to leave them both, I was exultant. I reflected on who out of the two taught me more and what was learnt. I must admit that it was the bad cop who educated me more. In addition to not using harmful speech as ill-spoken words could hurt, I realized the importance of fostering empathy when someone might be going through a tough time. As I have aged, I find his "used car" comments amusing. Perhaps, I should have responded with a wink and a smile, "I am not into used car drivers!" The look on his face would have been priceless to watch!

It is the difficult people who make us appreciate their opposites. I fully believe that people whom we find difficult show up like clockwork because they have something to teach us. The sooner we learn what they have arrived to teach us, the sooner they will depart.

While early on in my career, I was waiting in a lobby of a business to be called in for an interview. There was an Indian man in the lobby also waiting for someone. After some time, the manager arrived at the lobby and walked straight up to the awaiting man with his hand extended and said, "Welcome, Dr. Joshi. You can come in now." This man was embarrassed and told him that he was not Dr. Joshi. It did not occur to the manager that an Indian female sitting in the same room could also be Dr. Joshi. This was in the early 1990s; there still were not that many women with Ph.Ds. in the workforce.

Now, when I look around at my current workplace, more than 40% of the population consists of women. Many have doctorate degrees, and some hold director or higher-level positions. My bosses and colleagues are exceptional men and women. There are women executives in the conference rooms and in the board rooms of companies. The comments that I described from 30 years ago are not heard anymore, not at least at my workplace. How wonderful is that! I cannot forget, though, that where I work currently is a superb technology company! Is what I described at my current company the norm in all workplaces? Perhaps not, but I am hopeful that we are heading towards a better tomorrow no matter where we are employed!

Kiran Joshi, Ph.D.

There was a time when envy would set in when I would see men reaching higher up faster in their careers than me. I have come to an understanding that I can only rejoice in others' success while moving forward with my own efforts. I only have control over my own actions, and as Buddhist teachings say, we must not expect a standing ovation for our actions. I no longer cling to anything in return as it is the expectation that causes suffering. In fact, more started coming my way after I stopped stating my desires.

Occasionally, I get asked by my female colleagues how women can succeed in a workplace. To reach the executive level has required challenging work and emotional intelligence, along with technical strength. Persistence, respectfulness, full contribution to whatever needs to get done, committing to the work and delivering on time, and constantly seeking opportunities to improve are pillars of success for any human being, male or female.

Women must learn to trust their capabilities and move forward with confidence. As Sheryl Sandberg states so eloquently in her book, *Lean In*, "Sit at the table; seek and speak your truth."[2] As women professionals, I often notice that in meetings we sideline ourselves by taking a chair in a corner or in the back row, away from the center of power. We also have a habit of apologizing after stating our opinions. Why do we do that? Find your space on the table where you belong. State what you mean and let it be. We don't have to be at the two opposite ends of human personality – we don't need to swear like drunken sailors or be obnoxious to get our point across; neither do we need to act so meekly that we are invisible. Be authentic. Know your audience and be seen and heard as appropriate.

Finally, it does not matter what setting I am in, I do not bring my "womanhood" to a professional setting. Neither do I try to act like a man. I bring my whole self to the table.

Let us support each other, male or female, white, yellow, brown, or black along with all hues in between.

I am immensely grateful for how far women have come in professional fields due to our challenging work and persistence. I am also hopeful for what the future will bring. We must recognize though that we could not have done this without female role models who paved the path for us and without the support of the males in our lives. My father, brothers, husband, son, nephews, teachers, friends, bosses, and colleagues are marvelous men that I have tremendous respect for.

Kiran Joshi, Ph.D.

7. DON'T PUSH THE RIVER!

My husband was doing his postdoctoral work at AT&T Bell Labs in New Jersey. His research project was successful, and he landed an excellent job at Applied Materials, a semiconductor equipment manufacturing company, in Santa Clara, California, in 1993. Because our daughter was a baby, we decided that I would pursue a job search once we settled down at our home in California. I took delight in taking my daughter to the park and the pool where I met some wonderful moms with children of similar age; one of them became my lifelong friend that I cherish deeply.

A couple of months later, I began my job search. Hundreds of applications yielded no response. I signed up with a job placement firm paying them $5,000 to help me polish my resume and conduct some mock interviews. None of these efforts led to landing a job, and it was disheartening to say the least. Feeling dejected, I decided to complete the Environmental, Health, and Safety (EH&S) Certification through UC Santa Cruz. I do not remember how I became aware of this program. Although it was disappointing not to find a job after having a Ph.D. and postdoctoral experience, fate was taking me in a direction that I could not even have imagined. While completing the certification, I started volunteering with the City of Santa Clara Hazardous Materials Division, working on chemical management plans. Over the next few weeks, we were having dinner with some friends. There was a young man at the dinner unknown to us from Stanford University who put me in contact with the Stanford University Environmental Program manager. I was hired as a temporary employee at $10 an hour to assist with the chemical data management system. This work was far below my ability, but I was elated at this opportunity. The flexibility to adapt and be open to anything had been learnt many years ago when I immigrated to Canada.

Fairly soon after I arrived at Stanford, my supervisor commented that he was moving me to another manager who taught me the regulatory framework around environmental protection. His comment was quite humorous, in fact, when he broke the news to me, which was, "Why use a Rolls Royce where a Pinto will do." I excelled at what I did and relished the opportunities. I started gaining additional skills from others in the same department. I also continued to take relevant courses from UC Berkeley and UC Santa Cruz. Since it was a temporary position, I kept applying for EH&S jobs elsewhere. It was a hard

Kiran Joshi, Ph.D.

journey as I was overqualified for many of these positions. After countless applications, the first real opportunity came two years after starting my assignment at the university. It was at a company named Spectrian in Sunnyvale, California. When the time came for me to leave Stanford, the department leader met with me and described that he would have a senior level position very shortly and that he would contact me. I had made up my mind to leave as I saw the stagnation around me in the university's EH&S Department. I was too young and driven to stay there long-term. Stanford did call back, but I chose not to interview.

At Spectrian, the hiring manager had discarded my application with a big "NO" on it due to the Ph.D. degree; however, a junior level employee there who was entrusted with the EH&S responsibilities in addition to his own job asked him to interview me anyways. After a couple of meetings with them, I was hired. The employee told me later that he was frightened while doing the EH&S work since he was so underqualified, and he knew of the liability that he had been shouldered with. The company designed and manufactured highly linear radio frequency power amplifiers for wireless infrastructure equipment suppliers and was eventually bought by Cree, an East Coast firm. It had a small fab, R&D lab, and a manufacturing line. It was a first-rate learning place as I worked with some extremely intelligent people. I continued to take classes through UC and completed professional safety certification through an internationally recognized firm in the United States. I stayed at this company for about three years but got bored after a while.

This job was the springboard that I needed because I never had to apply for any other job from there on. The employers came looking for me from then on with a significant salary increase from the $10 an hour job that I had with Stanford University. Applied Materials, Solyndra (Solar), and Alta Devices (Solar) followed over the next few years. Every move led to more challenging work and with better titles and salaries. I eventually landed at QuantumScape, a solid-state battery company, in San Jose, where I have been for almost ten years. When I thought about these transitions through different companies, it was abundantly clear that every job came along because of the experience and connections at the previous company. Each opportunity was connected, and it taught me something rewarding and challenging about work and people. I spent time reflecting on what worked and what did not in the previous workplace so that I did not duplicate the negative circumstances in the next job.

Kiran Joshi, Ph.D.

Our son was born while I was working at Spectrian. My supervisor there was a nice man but a bit harsh if I ever needed time off to take care of my sick children. He did not even realize how his response was affecting me when children-related issues came up. Over time, I realized that it was a bit of a challenge for him to deal with a professional young mother. Remote work was not in anyone's vocabulary at that time. I could have talked to him, but confronting or challenging one's manager or someone in authority was not something that one did in the Indian culture, and this has been an issue for me throughout my career. Outside such challenges, I excelled in what I did at my job and was promoted a couple of levels, doubling my salary in three years.

The career moved on from semiconductor to solar to batteries as I wrote above. Other than Applied Materials, which is a large semiconductor company, the rest of the places that I worked at had fewer than 1,000 employees. Although Applied Materials was a great learning ground, smaller companies where personal connections can be made have been more enjoyable for me. Having a Ph.D. and doing EH&S was a blessing and a curse, as I thought from time to time. The curse was that the EH&S professionals often got looked at as support staff who deserved lower compensation compared to other professionals with

Ph.D.'s at companies. I have worked hard to make the management see the technical side of EH&S work. This discipline is embedded into every step at the workplace as a part of the overall risk management strategy of a company. EH&S is prominent in all aspects of a company operation including acquisition of a site, concept stage of the product, design, R&D and manufacturing, sales, product takeback programs, and site closure to name a few. I have succeeded at it in my current role. This will continue to benefit my colleagues now and those who will come after I am long gone. Especially at a battery company where chemical hazards abound, a Ph.D. chemist in the EH&S department has benefited the company and me. Having a Ph.D. is a blessing because I can talk to scientists at their level, which reduces any resistance to the proposed solutions. The professional degree and ability to engage with employees at all levels brings credibility and acknowledgement.

My professional journey has not been easy. At times, when I was submitting resumes early on in my career, comments such as "no one would hire you with this resume" or "you needed to know the regulatory citations by heart" were made. This was a major turn-off. I had to stop wasting my time with these people because it was just their opinion; their negativities were not going to be my reality. I feel that I have been a self-taught individual in this arena. In addition to technical capabilities, a few other factors which have helped me excel in my job are: 1) Working from the heart – if I make decisions which are based on risk assessment and practicality of implementation, these decisions will be proven right. 2) Getting to know the technology and people deeply – the goal has been to provide practical solutions that *enable* technology instead of being a roadblock while creating a safe environment for all. Being a chemist and doing a few other things well along with knowing the regulatory framework have been sufficient for me. Being an advocate for the employees to the management by educating the management on the importance of safe work practices has paid great dividends. Once the employees feel that their well-being is genuinely being addressed, there is nothing which they will not do for themselves, their co-workers, and the company.

I passionately believe that if a company can do EH&S well, it is highly likely that this will show up as an improvement in other aspects of its work, including employee morale and retention. This sentiment is fully understood by the QuantumScape management. It is also echoed in the book called "The Power of Habit" by Charles Duhigg.[1]

I have spent a significant amount of time discussing the importance of employees taking care of their own well-being and of everyone else who works with them. With the employees, I simply cannot help but touch on the fact that we tend to think that accidents happen to "others," but, if we are all on one team, there is no "other." Fostering such an environment among the team members has paid off well in both professional and personal satisfaction of the job well done.

I have often reflected on how to motivate 1,000 employees to do the right thing every single day. There are so many different personalities, how does one meet the need of each different type? I think that spending time to get to know what works for different personality types and presenting solutions accordingly has been beneficial.

Although I have done my job well, not all has been rosy, as some have felt that I am not controlling enough. That is not me

---

[1] Charles Duhigg, The Power of Habit, Random House, 2012, Random House, Chapter 4.

Kiran Joshi, Ph.D.

because it is below everyone's dignity to be treated like that. Unless it is a life-or-death situation, all work can be done from a place of care and compassion. We are who we are; compassion works for me!

The 2020 pandemic of COVID-19 presented a unique challenge to keep the workplace open and functioning, yet not have the employees fall sick. Due to personal connections with the management and the employees, I was able to devise and implement practices which kept a COVID-19 outbreak from occurring at the worksite. There was hardly any information in the early days when the COVID-19 virus was declared a pandemic. The employees put in heroic efforts by adhering to the use of uncomfortable personal protective equipment while remaining committed to moving the work forward. I have no doubt that this would not have been possible unless the workplace already had an established culture of a safe environment.

Although I have ventured into patent law, quality, and a few other areas at the workplace, I have realized that environmental protection, occupational safety, and worker health are my calling, and this job is rewarding. When I was pushing the river in the direction my career was not supposed to go, nothing was working. Now, I do get paid at par; in addition, my degree has given me the opportunity to make decisions which have kept people safe from chemical and other hazards while moving the technology initiatives forward. I will never know how many injuries have been prevented or lives saved due to my work; knowing that I am effective in my job, and that I can inspire employees to go home to their families without being hurt means a lot to me. This is, indeed, my purpose on earth.

I also recognize that my work has involved controlling emissions to the environment which means clean air to breathe and clean water to drink for all. Proper chemical management in my job means smaller volumes of chemicals going to landfill, incinerators, and treatment plants. Addition of sustainability to EH&S has broadened my horizons in circular economy and reduction in greenhouse gas emissions. My job is a calling as it both protects the earth and allows employees to work safely while moving revolutionary technology forward. As I have matured, I have really started understanding the importance of my work and embraced it wholeheartedly. I am contented and grateful in the current role which has allowed me to marry my education with the advancement of technology in a safe manner.

Kiran Joshi, Ph.D.

8. THE BALANCING ACT

I often get asked how I balanced having children and a full-time career. I didn't. I was young, ambitious, and married to a man whose work required long hours and frequent travel for many years. I was trying to be the best employee, best mother, best wife, and best housekeeper. It took its toll on my health as migraines were frequent. If I were to redo my life, I would worry less about being the best at everything. My career has progressed while my children have grown up to be excellent citizens. I would remain unconcerned about how the house looked when visitors came.

First and foremost, what assisted me tremendously as a young professional mom was a partner who participated whole-heartedly in both home and childcare. He took care of the children in the morning and dropped them at school or day care, and I did the evening pickups along with meals and activities including homework. We hired help where needed. I fully realize the blessing of a supportive partner along with the ability to hire a helping hand and acknowledge that not everyone may be facing such circumstances for many different reasons.

I could not have married a better man; his virtuous qualities have grown on me over time. There is no anger or aversion in him. He holds no grudges. He loves and respects all life. He gives freely without any expectation in return. He does not have the desire to accumulate. He does not talk just for the sake of talking or embellish his accomplishments. These are the qualities that Buddha's teachings say we cultivate. The American workplace, unfortunately, puts emphasis on bravado. Even at social gatherings, some people do not talk to him because he is not busy making small talk. None of this bothers him but I used to notice it. It does not bother me anymore - I have learnt the art of "being" from him. He has taught me that "success" is not one's title, money, or material possessions; it is being able to sleep peacefully at night after an honest day of work.

When I was a young mother, I had anxiety about getting to work early so that I could return early to take care of the children. This was no way to live as I was always on the go. I made an active effort of reading and listening to teachers such as Wayne Dyer, Thich Nhat Hanh, and Pema Chodron. Their talks were inspiring. I memorized Guru Nanak Dev's chanting of "Ik Onkar" (Guru Nanak Ji 's teaching which means that there is only one God, and that is the eternal truth) which helped me navigate the early mornings. Meditation and deep diaphragm breathing from Sri Sri Ravi Shankar helped immensely too. Breathing while looking at the sun with eyes closed and focusing on loosening my forehead and jaw a few times a day was extremely beneficial while I was at work. Over time, it became clear that the anxiety was coming from the fact that I was trying to control what the day would bring. Accepting that I could only do my best from the place of compassion for myself and everyone else, and that there was truly little control over what life would bring my way, was extremely freeing.

None of this was easy as I still lapsed back into the "control" mode, but I was more aware of it as time passed. Instead of reacting to a situation, the impact of just waiting a few minutes and acting from a place of innate intelligence and compassion for all sides helped. When difficult situations arose, it was obvious that I needed to stop judging the motivation of other individuals as they were also trying to do their best from where they were. I also started asking myself, "What if my perception is wrong?" And often it was.

Faith and Perseverance – My Journey

Our children have grown up. We did not push them to become anything specific when they were little. We exposed them to different art and athletic activities in addition to working with them on their studies and doing extra math and reading. They knew the importance of education and worked hard. We allowed them social freedom to develop good friendships, but we made a point of knowing their friends.

While attending classes at Swami Chinmayananda's mission in San Jose, the teachers would often quote Swami Ji's saying about children, "Children are not vessels to be filled, but lamps to be lit," which had impact on how we viewed our children. Khalil Gibran's poem also spoke powerfully to me on child rearing:

> *"They are the sons and daughters of Life's longing*
> *for itself.*
> *They come through you but not from you,*
> *And though they are with you, yet they belong not to you."*[3]

We tried to be mindful of letting the children develop their own individuality instead of having our unfulfilled ambitions come true through them.

Kiran Joshi, Ph.D.

For a long time, I felt guilty about not being able to spend more time with my son when he was little since he did not like being in childcare centers. After he grew up, I apologized to him for not being there for him as much as I thought he would have wanted me to. His response was very loving as he told me that he did not think that I was not there for him. It was a challenge to accept that I could not be in two places simultaneously – with my children, whom I loved beyond words, and the job at which I was good! Both my children have grown up to be independent individuals as they learned to cook at a young age, do their own laundry, and manage their own affairs since I was not always there. I did what had to be done.

Over time, I have come to realize that life is not a balancing act on a teeter-totter because I am constantly falling; instead, I must focus on what needs to be done at this time. When I am at work, I am fully committed to work. When I am at home, I am there. As I have aged, I have also stopped worrying about what anyone has to say or think if I leave a bit earlier from work to exercise or take care of what needed to be done outside work. I have also stopped trying to live a life of perfection. It is a trap – for overachieving working mothers, my advice is to stop trying to create a life in which there is a perfect husband, perfect house, perfect children, perfect job, and perfect you. This is a recipe for disaster as such lives and people do not exist. It is not worth wasting energy and driving ourselves and our loved ones crazy. Perfection means "the end" or "achieved." Why would I want "the end"! The "imperfections" of our lives make us vulnerable, and there is beauty in that web. We are enough as we are. We have come into this body and life span with our measures of happiness and sorrow. Although we want to step in and take away our loved one's difficulties, it is their burden. We must be present to support them, but we must not try to live for them. Life is truly a remarkable gift. Enjoy it because it will not last. Getting to this understanding has not been easy. It has taken a lifetime to put these learnings into practice.

I just am when I am at work. And I just am when I am away from work. Life has become more enjoyable to live this way.

When life starts getting difficult, these sayings from Rumi at my work desk inspire me (a wall hanging purchased in Konya, Turkey):

Kiran Joshi, Ph.D.

Seven Advice of Mevlana Rumi

1. *In generosity and helping others*

    BE LIKE A RIVER

2. *In compassion and grace*

    BE LIKE THE SUN

3. *In concealing others' faults*

    BE LIKE NIGHT

4. *In anger and fury*

    BE LIKE DEAD

5. *In modesty and humanity*

    BE LIKE EARTH

6. *In tolerance*

    BE LIKE SUN

7. *EITHER EXIST AS YOU ARE*

    OR BE AS YOU LOOK

I aspire to live this advice. Although I fail often, I dust myself off and work on not repeating the same. I am wise one moment and a fool the next, and that is ok too!

9. REALIZING PEACE

For almost ten years, I have been working at a lithium metal battery company. The technology is revolutionary. There are no set standards that I could apply in this job. A lot of work has been done using risk management principles. At times, I feel like I am at the leading edge of the lithium battery health and safety field. There are new learnings and challenges on a routine basis. Although I have come far at my workplace, at times I feel that I know so little! There is a lot that has been done, and yet there is a lot more to do. This was the first company that was looking for a Ph.D. to run its EH&S programs. I still did not apply for the job until the company representative called me. This opportunity has provided immense understanding, teaching, and leadership opportunities. I have reached the pinnacle of my career here and would not trade it for any other place.

Silicon Valley is the hub of innovation and reaping financial rewards for the demanding work through IPOs and stock incentives. When my chance to make money arrived in 2021, I did not take advantage of selling the shares. Partly due to the

Faith and Perseverance - My Journey

Russia/Ukraine war, inflation, and supply chain issues related to the COVID-19 pandemic, the stock price plunged. As the stock price decreased, anxiety started rearing its head. It became clear to me that I was caught in a certain expectation of earnings which brought me to the wheel of "samsara" (aimless existence in the world of material things and suffering) and kept me there. I had to suffer the consequences of attachment and expectations or let it all go. Really paying attention to the times when I was feverish about the stock price and sale, it was obvious what had to be done. I let it go. Joseph Goldstein's wisdom played a crucial role as I started noting when "Mara" (the God of desire) visited me many times a day. As I became more aware of how the wheel of the samsara was yanking me around, I wanted to get off it. It felt like Mara had permanently moved in with me. In fact, I had become Mara! Now, this suffering of the mind was more intense than any physical suffering of the cancer treatment.

Here, I quote the poem from Danna Faulds called "Let It Go" which stays at my desk (added here with permission from Ms. Faulds; reference provided)[4]:

Let It Go

Let go of the ways you thought life
would unfold; the holding of plans
or dreams or expectations – Let it
all go. Save your strength to swim
with the tide. The choice to fight
what is here before you now will
only result in struggle, fear, and
desperate attempts to flee from the
very energy you long for. Let go.
Let it all go and flow with the grace
that washes through your days whether
you receive it gently or with all your
quills raised to defend against invaders.
Take this on faith: the mind may never
find the explanations that it seeks, but
you will move forward nonetheless.
Let go, and the wave's crest will carry
you to unknown shores, beyond your
wildest dreams or destinations. Let it
all go and find the place of rest and
peace, and certain transformation.

Faith and Perseverance - My Journey

I am more at peace now that I can flag when certain unwanted thoughts arise. These tendencies are still there but now I let them come and I let them go. I am not attached to a certain outcome. Whatever happens, so be it. I am working on being with what is here. Life has offered so much; there is nothing to be worried about. Nothing really matters as whatever we gather disperses at the end. It is not a defeatist view of life, and it is not that I do not continue to work hard; instead, it is contentment with what is here and now.

I continue to expose myself to spiritual books and talks from authors and speakers on Hinduism and Buddhism, along with literature from Native American and Western philosophers. The book by Native American author Joseph M. Marshall called "Keep Going: The Art of Perseverance" remains my favorite. It has touched me deeply as a grandfather tells stories of perseverance and strength to his grandson. I fully intend to read this book to my grandchildren many times over when the time comes.

Kiran Joshi, Ph.D.

The advent of podcasts has me hooked on Joseph Goldstein's[2] and Jack Kornfield's[3] talks. I spend at least an hour a day listening while driving, walking, or at the gym. During drives, I used to focus on the daily news until I realized that so much news consumption was hurting my mental health. Now, the Buddhist podcasts are life savers. While Joseph's talks focus on the non-self and are on Buddhist Suttas and philosophy, I love how Jack weaves in many stories on related topics in his talks. I need to listen to both speakers to maintain balance in my mind. Joseph Goldstein's podcasts give me knowledge of Buddha's Suttas and mindfulness, while Jack Kornfield's talks keep the love alive. While being exposed to such great speakers and authors, I have tried meditation practice. Sitting at one place and meditating does not work for me all the time. However, I get the best experience of meditation when I am on an exercise machine or walking. It is my mind and me. If this is how my meditation practice is going to be in this life, I fully accept that. Being kind in my verbal and written speech is also a form of meditation that I pay a lot of attention to.

---

[2]: Joseph Goldstein's Podcasts: Insight Hour Podcast with Joseph Goldstein

[3]: Jack Kornfield's Podcasts: Heart Wisdom Podcast with Jack Kornfield

Meditative experiences are difficult to repeat and describe; one can only be in them, not of them. Sri Sri Ravi Shankar's meditative practices around yoga and deep breathing followed by meditation have helped. I share one experience here where I lay down during one of his meditation sessions. Once the yoga and deep breathing session were over, we were instructed to lie down with a blanket or something warm on ourselves. In this posture, after a few seconds, there was an immense sensation of golden light enveloping me. It was extremely soothing. As I let go increasingly, my relatives, both alive and from the past, started appearing and disappearing in my vision. I felt such love for them that tears were flowing profusely down my face. This sense was so profound that it left me feeling that nothing but love mattered in the Universe. The light slowly subsided and the feeling diminished. But I was changed forever.

From being steeped into spirituality, what has also been learnt is to recognize the one nature of all life. In public settings, it is easy now to let go of what I may not like about someone's action; we are all just fulfilling our karma and life's mission. Now, I find myself saying "May you be peaceful" to whoever I see on the road. It has become easier to be with myself. Now, when I think of all life, it really does include all life, including

Kiran Joshi, Ph.D.

animals, bugs, plants, trees, and minerals, not just human beings.

Going back to my childhood prayer and expanding upon it based on what life has taught me, I recite the following prayer often:

May I be peaceful;

May I be loving;

May I be without fears and worries;

May I give freely without any expectation;

May I be surrounded and protected by the Universal light;

May all of creation be surrounded and protected

by the Universal light!

Sometimes, I switch the "I" in the above prayer with a "name" depending on whom I am praying for. Sometimes when I wake up during the night, I find myself reciting this prayer for someone who may have tried to cause harm in the past. My ego jumps in where I question why I am praying for this individual! I get a chuckle as I observe this thought. This prayer plays in the background of my mind throughout the day and at night without an effort. The question of "Who Am I" has been answered by the first two lines of the prayer – I am a peaceful and loving soul. This is the same soul that dwells in all life. This realization brings a sense of reverence towards all life.

From time to time, an intense feeling that I am the Universe takes over just to dissolve into that I am nothing. One may experience this state during meditation as the golden light surrounds one just to disappear in a point form, and then to rise and dissolve cyclically. We gather and we disperse. In a non-meditative state, it is a struggle at times to hold onto these states, especially when life's challenges test me. I am not perfect and neither do I really want to be. Nor do I hold anyone else to any standards as the thought is that we are all beautiful as we are.

As I head towards the later years of life, the goal is to live peacefully. I do my part whole heartedly, and whatever life offers me, the response is "this too!" This life has been a fulfilling journey. There is nothing to worry about based on past experiences. If my actions are supporting my goal of living peacefully, I am marching in the right direction.

Kiran Joshi, Ph.D.

As the journey of life continues, it is abundantly clear that all events fit, even the unpleasant ones, but isn't what I thought was unpleasant, a fertile ground for spiritual growth?

May we see the futile nature of our egos and individual existence which causes so much harm including war and destruction!

May all beings be peaceful!
May we see divinity in all!

The Journey Continues!...

Kiran Joshi, Ph.D.

REFERENCES & GLOSSARY

REFERENCES:

1. Kornfield, J., & Grynberg, S. (2023, April 12). *Heart Wisdom with Jack Kornfield* (No. 183) https://podcasts.apple.com/us/podcast/heart-wisdom-with-jack-kornfield/id923017416
2. Sandberg, S. (2015) *Lean In: Women, Work, and The Will To Lead*: First Edition, Alfred A. Knopf, New York.
3. Gibran, K. (1923) *The Prophet*: Alfred A. Knopf, New York, p. 17.
4. Faulds, D. (2002) *Poems from the Heart of Yoga: Go In and In*: First Edition, Peaceable Kingdom Books, Virginia, p. 48.

GLOSSARY:

1. *BCIT* – British Columbia Institute of Technology located in Burnaby, BC, Canada
2. *Bhagavad Geeta* – The Song of Lord, ancient Indian scripture
3. *BRCA1* – *Br*east *Ca*ncer Gene; harmful mutations in this gene have been correlated to many different cancers https://www.cancer.gov/about-cancer/causes-prevention/genetics/brca-fact-sheet
4. *Buddha* – Enlightened One
5. *CA* – California
6. *Choohlah* – A rudimentary clay oven
7. *COVID*-19 – Coronavirus disease
8. *Diwali* – The "Festival of Lights" celebrated in fall when God Rama returned to His kingdom after fourteen years of exile and after defeating the Demon God, Ravana
9. *EH&S* – *E*nvironmental Protection, Worker *H*ealth & Occupational *S*afety
10. *EHSS* – *E*nvironment Protection, Worker *H*ealth, Occupational *S*afety, and *S*ustainability
11. *ESL* – English as a Second Language
12. *Gurbani* – Teachings from Guru Granth Sahib
13. *Gurudwara* – Sikh Temple
14. *Guru Granth Sahib* – Sikh Holy Book
15. *IIT* – Indian Institute of Technology located in many cities of India
16. *Ik Onkar* – There is one God
17. *IPO* – Initial public offering of stocks
18. *Ji* – Suffix that implies respect
19. *Kirtan* – Devotional singing

20. *Mahabharata* – One of the two major epics of ancient India
21. *Mara* – Buddhist God of death, rebirth, and desire who tried to tempt Buddha the night of His enlightenment
22. *Mera Naam Joker* – My Name is Joker, Indian movie from 1970 by R.K. Films
23. *Peepal Tree* – Ficus religiosa tree
24. *Ph. D.* – Doctor of Philosophy
25. *Pooja* – Hindu prayers
26. *Ramayana* – One of the two major epics of ancient India
27. *Sadhu* – Holy man
28. *Samsara* – Aimless existence in the world of material things and suffering according to Buddhism
29. *Satvik* – Virtuous or pure
30. *Swami* – Master of himself
31. *SFU* – Simon Fraser University located in Burnaby, BC, Canada
32. *UBC* – University of British Columbia located in Vancouver, BC, Canada
33. *UC* – University of California
34. *US* – United States of America

Kiran Joshi, Ph.D.

ACKNOWLEDGMENTS

This book has been in the making for the past five years. I am indebted to people who inquired about various phases of my life and encouraged me to put it down in a book. This book went through many iterations with the help of family members, friends, and colleagues. They provided the input yet allowed me to not lose my voice. The artwork is by people dear to me who have their own full-time jobs and obligations. With much gratitude to such a wonderful and supportive community.

www.ingramcontent.com/pod-product-compliance
Lightning Source LLC
Chambersburg PA
CBHW072234150726
48002CB00005B/2086